Global Graphics: **Color**

A Guide to Design with Color
for an International Market

L.K. Peterson

·

Cheryl Dangel Cullen

GLOUCESTER MASSACHUSETTS

ROCKPORT
PUBLISHERS

How to Use This Book

The book is organized by continent, region, and then country. Color traditions are noted within each country, along with information on the historical significance of many of the colors that are followed today, as well as anecdotal notes on colors that are taboo or that have given rise to new associations in recent years, such as the red AIDS ribbon. This information is followed by actual examples of designs, culled from design studios the world over, that were created with these color associations in mind. We've tried to include mention of as many countries and their cultural color differences as possible.

Contents

Introduction

In the same way that language, music, and food differ from one culture to the next, so does the significance and meaning attached to colors. We react daily to countless color-coded messages, having learned from early childhood which colors signal stop or go or wait. And color has dozens of other associative meanings, from the monumental to the mundane, that we take utterly for granted and accept as fact.

A single color can have very different meanings in different cultures. In Asia orange is a positive, spiritually enlightened, and life-affirming color, while in the US it is a sign of road hazards, traffic delays, and fast-food restaurants. Colors can symbolize a rite of passage, differentiate a premium from a discount brand, and distinguish between fun and serious, young and old, male and female. Context is everything: A group of people wearing black might be the crowd at a gallery opening, priests, Mennonites, a punk band, ninjas, Kabuki stagehands, Bedouins, mourners, or a mime troupe. A red five-pointed star might be the marking of a Chinese fighter jet, part of the logo for Macy's department store, or a Heineken Beer label. But beware—a little bit of context isn't always enough to go on.

Even the colors of nature are subject to regional context. The sky is blue everywhere but—depending upon where you live—a clear blue sky might be a predictable daily occurrence or a noteworthy break in the typical cloud cover. A spot of green might be an oasis in t he desert or a patch of moss in a rainforest. Red, while universally equated with blood, can signify the courage of heroes or the slaughter of martyrs. Because of their innate rarity, minerals have a fairly consistent hierarchy of value throughout the world, best exemplified by the gold, silver, and bronze of Olympic medals.

The multifaceted meaning of color is good news for designers; among the tremendous differences and variety of color associations worldwide, there are few outright taboos. While this doesn't mean that anything goes, it does signal that design needn't be bland or insipid to avoid offending anybody. The challenge is that every culture has multiple layers of meaning, and many subtle conflicting and contradictory significances regarding color, from traditional colors associated with birth, weddings, and funerals to the colors of the taxicabs and mailboxes. In addition, even the farthest corners of the world are exposed to the visual Esperanto of multinational marketing and communication. Coca-Cola red, Kodak yellow, and IBM blue are recognizable everywhere.

The Pantone Color Matching System allows for precise specifications of color. Socio X's covers for the Pantone textile color books hint at the hues within. One of the most popular color matching systems used worldwide, Pantone represents a consensus necessitated by the global marketplace and the need for recognized standards of color. While it allows for clear specification of color, it cannot articulate color's many implications.

"Think global, hire local," is an ideal most designers might dream about, but few have the resources to afford that luxury. Once the specialty of a few advertising agencies with international sweep, cross-cultural design is now an everyday event for firms of all sizes. Simply designing a Web site engages an international market: Anyone in the world can log on and see what's been created.

For the most part, this book is descriptive, not prescriptive. Too many variables exist for any one-size-fits-all answers. Offered is a framework of information from which one can make an informed and appropriate color choice when designing cross-culturally. The design answers are sometimes elusive; Global Graphics: Color can arm you with the right questions to ask. For each country included, the customary significance of color is detailed and social context, historical information, and aesthetic background are provided. Where noteworthy and illuminating, the origin or development of a color meaning's is described.

In conversations with dozens of designers experienced in cross cultural projects, several choice bits of general advice have been gathered: Be yourself (mostly). While breaking the rules may be the best solution, find out what the rules are first. An appetite for novelty and the exotic is fairly universal, so don't "go native"; however well-intentioned, this actually runs a higher risk of being offensive than does completely ignoring local customs. Being aware of and sensitive to regional preferences doesn't mean mimicking them. It is important to note that in much of the world, whether a surface is wet or dry, glossy or matte is as important as its hue. Pay literal attention to the local color. What is the color of the landscape? What colors are houses painted? What colors do the inhabitants wear? What colors are used in traditional crafts? The color or colors you need may not be among these, but you'll understand the color vernacular familiar to the audience you are trying to reach.

North America

Among market researchers, the Luscher Color Test, which links color to psychology, is held to be somewhere between Indispensable Guideline and Gospel Truth. While useful as a starting point, exclusive reliance on this or any scientific or psychological system of color meaning overlooks the importance of individual experience, personal preference, and a host of other variables. Following conventional color codes and defying them have both been done successfully.

Americans and Canadians display a preference for subdued, traditional, safe colors on items that are expensive or intended to last—cars, houses, and furniture, or costly formal clothing. Brighter colors are reserved for accents. Moreover, the further south you head, the brighter the colors as evidenced by Mexico's colorful palette. Still, even "durable goods" such as automobiles are subject to fashion swings. The two-toned American cars of the 1950s sported colors, now synonymous with that era, that have not been used since. A brief vogue in the 1960s for large household appliances in "avocado green" and "harvest gold" is now remembered with embarrassment, although at the time they satisfied an appetite for any alternative to white. Whether a form of planned obsolescence or a momentary lapse in taste, the designer colors of today tend to turn up as tomorrow's white elephant. Conversely, fashionable colors are acceptable and desirable in goods that are small, inexpensive, or meant to last a relatively short time.

Advances in science and technology also impact color trends. Many products were redesigned in the 1950s to be visible on the blurry television broadcasts of the day; the color and design of the Marlboro cigarette box was created because it held up so well in black and white. Two generations of Americans have grown up watching the world on color televisions; another generation has grown up playing computer games; both have created a vivid, backlit color language unique to video monitors and virtual reality.

United States and Canada

Context means everything when using color in the US and Canada.

Red, white, and blue are the colors of the U.S. flag and the signature colors of the country. While overuse has diminished the impact of the three colors together, they still have patriotic punch. During the 1988 U.S. presidential campaign, one political party's convention hall was decorated in soft, pale shades of red, blue, and beige. The opposition labeled them "Pastel Patriots," implying that they were less than truly American, with the added implication that pastel colors are usually considered effeminate.

Red and white are the national colors of Canada, but the flag's maple leaf is surrounded by more than just white: There is a myth that the points of the leaf represent the ten Canadian provinces. But this is just folklore and, besides, the leaf has eleven points.

Do you think color isn't meaningful in the secular, commercial United States or its more polite neighbor, Canada? Go to a sporting event wearing the visiting team's colors; send out pink cards announcing the birth of a baby boy; or try finding a green stop sign, a blue fire truck, or a yellow Christmas tree. In the U.S. and Canada, color use may not follow any single, formal, codified system of meaning and symbolism; so context is everything. The commercial marketplace is where most color associative meanings came from in the first place, but marketing isn't color's only role in American society. States, cities, schools, sports teams, and street gangs, along with companies big and small, have signature colors.

Overall there are only minor differences between American and Canadian color conventions. In designing for Quebec, look to the historic colors of France and anticipate accommodating bilingual copy.

Meant as a warning or an invitation (and often both), red always draws attention to itself. Considered a loud color, red promises excitement; it is a powerful symbol of vibrancy and life, but also of danger and death. For women, high-heeled red shoes, red lipstick and red dresses are emblematic of sexiness and passion; for men, a red sports car functions in the same way (although a red sports car driven by a middle aged man is a virtual announcement of mid-life crisis). Red is also the color of adultery as immortalized in Nathaniel Hawthorne's novel, *A Scarlet Letter*. For all its implied thrill-seeking, however, red is also the color of safety or rescue (fire engines, emergency equipment). By a wide margin, Americans prefer red apples to green. In other foods, red is used to indicate hot and spicy flavors. In American academia, scarlet signals theology; crimson, journalism. Red, a brilliant scarlet, is the signature color of Canada. It is the color of the Canadian flag, and is the iconic color of the dress uniform of the Royal Canadian Mounted Police.

Yellow is the most visible color from a distance, sometimes to its detriment; thanks to a popular notion that visibility alone trumps good design, yellow can seem cheap. In the U.S., yellow is a cautionary signal; it once designated quarantine, and yellow tape is still used to cordon off areas under police investigation. Alternating black and yellow diagonal stripes indicate a hazardous area and are commonly seen around construction sites where heavy machinery is being operated; yellow is frequently paired with red on roadside signage. Long in use for marine safety equipment, protective or waterproof casings of bright yellow indicate that a camera or other item is meant for use under rough conditions. In most American cities, taxis are yellow. For the most part, this hue is considered to be a happy color, connoting the sun, welcome warmth, and ripe grains. According to the Luscher Color Test, yellow represents "spontaneity," is "expansive, aspiring, active, and investigatory," and signals "originality, expectancy, variability, and exhilaration."

On the downside, yellow in the English language has a host of negative connotations. The word yellow is synonymous with coward, while yellow journalism means biased, partisan, and inflammatory news reporting.

A popular hue, blue is the favorite of companies and organizations who wish to convey their reliability and trustworthiness; they are "true blue"—even if a bit cold, stiff, and probably not very exciting. Blue indicates quality, value, durability, strength, and authority. Dark blue is the color of officialdom. Uniforms, mailboxes, and symbols of the U.S. government are navy to midnight blue. Despite gray flannel's iconic status as the very definition of corporate conformity, dark blue suits are the daily uniform of office workers nationwide, while blue denim is everyday wear for people of all ages and sexes. In American academia, blue is the color of the study of philosophy, a reflection of the soothing, contemplative aspects of this hue. Expressions that contain blue can have high (blue ribbon, blue chip, blue blood) or low (blue humor, singing the blues) connotations.

Green is the color of money and nature, two things close to the hearts of Americans and Canadians. Newly a symbol of environmentalism, green has always been linked with forests, crops, and plentiful harvests, and in marketing or packaging signals things that are "all natural." Dark greens are considered outdoorsy and masculine, a favorite choice for automobiles. Vibrant kelly green is virtually synonymous with Ireland, important considering the large Irish-American population. In food, green indicates freshness, health, and mint flavor. As it gets paler, green gets less appealing. On its way to yellow, green takes on sickly and unpleasant associations—slime, bile, disease. Because of its recessive, allegedly calming nature, a flat, grayish green—dubbed "Institutional Green"—has become the unofficial color for the hallways of public schools in poor neighborhoods, the lobbies of post offices, and underfunded municipal agencies. Green is the common background color for highway signs. In academia, green is the color of medical studies. Some of the hue's more noteworthy negative meanings include envy, jealousy, disgrace, moral degradation, and inexperience.

Americans claim a strong dislike of orange, and yet the hue is everywhere. It has its good points: sunsets, citrus, flowers, and fall foliage; however, it is also associated with cheap molded plastic furniture, fast food restaurants, and other aesthetic blights. Used for signs on highway construction and maintenance, orange indicates not danger, but inconvenience and delay. Visibility is its key attribute: Conical road markers and vests worn by road crews are a dense deep orange. In much of the U.S., jailed prisoners are made to wear orange (an unintended throwback to the orange worn by Indian convicts that inspired the Buddha to wear orange robes). Orange also has industrial, mechanical implications, signaling the dangerous parts of machinery or energized equipment. More recently, orange has gained popularity—even as a corporate color—because of it is seen as a refreshing and invigorating change from the norm.

Purple's status as the color of nobility got tossed aside along with other trappings of European aristocratic hierarchy. The color is still linked to noble actions, however; the Purple Heart is a

THE ABSENCE OF COLOR

In the early 1990s, a variety of clear products were introduced, intended as a nod toward environmentalism. Although the colors were mostly superfluous to begin with, the public did not rush to embrace cola that was not brown and colorless mascara that didn't darken lashes, but made them appear "natural."

WEARING OF COLORS

The success of the AIDS ribbon has prompted a range of commemorative ribbons to symbolize different causes; but it wasn't the first "wearing of colors" in the U.S. Yellow ribbons have been tokens of remembrance for absent loved once since the 19th century, when the wives of U.S. Cavalry officers on duty in the Western frontier wore scarves of their husbands' regimental colors. The 1948 film *She Wore a Yellow Ribbon*, starring John Wayne, cemented the tradition in the 20th century. In the 1970s, the pop song *Tie A Yellow Ribbon* added the twist of a yellow ribbon signifying a welcome home, and although completely unofficial, yellow ribbons became a powerful symbol of remembrance for hostages held in the U.S. embassy in Iran in 1980. They are now routinely displayed as tokens signifying hope for the safe return of soldiers abroad.

FOOD AND FOOD PACKAGING

In food and food packaging, the overall rule is the deeper or darker the color, the stronger the flavor. This holds true for most food groups, and emerges from the appearance of food when it is at its best. Red means meat, green means vegetables, white means dairy. Golden brown implies grains, potatoes, bread, pastas, and nuts, and dark brown is inescapably linked with coffee and chocolate. Besides milk and eggs, white also signifies refinement and delicacy; white flour, sugar, rice, etc. Beer and ale are also color coded light to dark, from pilsners to stout.

Since much processed food isn't visible and is often no longer in its original form, buyers are all the more dependent upon a label's subtle and not-so-subtle signals about what is contained inside. Merely illustrating the contents either as before (a picture of a cow) or after (a picture of a steak) isn't always possible and is not necessarily the best solution. Where image is as much an element as the product, color plays a critical role. Black and gold indicate luxury, a premium product (worth a higher price); bright multi-colored packages mean fun, probably snack food. Earthy tones imply heartiness and health, as in grain products, or honey; green has come to mean not only vegetables but anything that is healthy and eco-friendly. Packaging that echoes the color (or desired color) of the ingredients is still popular, but often takes a back seat to a unifying brand identity and the need to stand out from the competition.

medal given to U.S. military personnel wounded or killed in battle. As a background color, purple can greatly amplify colors around it, and is often used for type. In a daring move, the company Federal Express used purple and orange—two rather unpopular colors—for its logo and corporate identity. In academia, purple is the color of the study of law, and is a popular favorite school color of many colleges and universities. In the English language, purple usually signals an excess of something better done in small portions; purple prose for example is embarrassingly melodramatic.

Pink is a highly changeable color. It can be warm or cool, quiet or loud. It is a decidedly feminine and sensuous color, and is usually described in the terminology of idealized femininity; it is the traditional color for baby girls. It is also the color of childhood; pink bestows cuteness in most any context. Intense "hot pink" signals fun and frivolity for all ages. Pink confections are especially sweet—cotton candy and bubble gum—but in most foods pink indicates a delicate flavor. Ironically the leading U.S. indigestion remedy, Pepto-Bismol, is pink. In recent years, pink (particularly a pink triangle) has become identified with the gay rights movement.

For most, brown is dull, boring, and prosaic—a sort of lack of color. But brown also has strong, earthy, dependable associations. The corporate color of the United Parcel Service is brown, as are National Park Service signs. Dark brown indicates rich, fertile soil and is frequently used in packaging coffee. Brown paper and cardboard have a myriad of meanings; inherent strength is generally one of them. Off-white or brownish paper is perceived as sturdier than white paper, and feels recycled and eco-friendly. Weighty medium to pale brown wrapping paper promises something exciting concealed; that the contents might be somehow forbidden and titillating stems from the tradition of illicit erotica being sent in "plain brown wrappers" to avoid seizure by postal officials. Brown also implies unprocessed (as in rice) and therefore healthy. On the negative side, brown conjures up images of barrenness, poverty, and rust.

Americans and Canadians prefer their gold stacked neatly in bank vaults, and when used as adornment, used sparingly and with great discretion on something truly deserving the honor— it is as if gold is just too precious to waste on decoration. The exception is in architecture, in which gilded domes and interiors are admissible. The excessive use of gold—gold jewelry, gold teeth, and gold-plated chrome on automobiles—has become associated with inner-city gangster culture and rap music. This region prefers a pale, champagne gold color to the darker gold favored by most Asians and Italians. The glowing, luminous quality of gold adds a fine aspect to the marketing of luxury items like cosmetics, chocolate, or liquor; it conveys a sense of quality. Together, the colors black and gold signal opulence and grandeur.

While it is not exclusively linked to death, black does have decidedly somber associations; it implies morbidity, despair, the void, evil, sin, and negation. The black holes of outer space are a metaphor for absolute nothingness. Black commands respect; it is meant to be taken seriously. Black means business. Black is perennially chic, sophisticated, dignified, dramatic, very adult, and extremely formal. Because it is the absence of color, the surface texture of black is noteworthy. Matte black implies something sturdy and industrial, high-tech, and stately; gloss black is sleek and powerful, with a hint of danger or malevolence. Black also tends to be sexy.

Like black, white has many paradoxical symbolic connotations for Americans; it can mean clean, sanitary, pure, elegant, and perfect. It can also mean cold, antiseptic, empty, ghostly, boring, and unfinished. Like gray and brown, the word white by itself is deceptively simple. This umbrella term covers a range of subtle tones from bright white to beige and cream. It is the preferred color for blank paper, despite design inroads made by recycled off-whites and browns. Unless attention is deliberately brought to a white background, it will go unnoticed. White is the academic color of the arts and calls up a newly painted room, a blank canvas, clean sheets—white means new, fresh, and ready to go.

Combining utilitarianism, craftsmanship, and the inherent value of the substance itself, silver is a favorite. With metallic colors, texture is important; when it is shiny and highly reflective—a silver tea service, the chrome of an automobile bumper—it feels sleek, classy, and expensive. A matte or brushed finish—like a Zippo lighter or experimental airplane—reads as modern, high-tech, virile, and built for speed. A metallic look is considered masculine, and is often seen on traditionally male-oriented products, from tools to toiletries. Generally speaking, the lighter gray the metallic color, the more upscale (silver, steel, and chrome). The darker gray, the humbler the material (aluminum, pewter, and zinc).

Even more than brown, gray is considered a non-color. It is associated with humility, winter, grief, penitence, inertia, and depression. This combination of black and white, however, offers a rich diversity of tones and has many positive meanings. Strength and durability (stone, steel, concrete) can be conveyed with gray. As a background, gray can subdue or amplify other colors; as type or a foreground element, it can subtly add depth and dimension to design. Gray is a color greatly affected by texture. Charcoal gray clothing is staid, elegant, and traditional—above the fray of fashion trends. Gray hair (and gray in general) confers maturity and wisdom.

IS BLUE TABOO?

Blue food is rare, but the color is frequently seen on labels and packaging owing to its popularity and versatility. Used mostly on dairy products, candies, and sweeteners, blue often connotes some variation on a strong flavor—decaffeinated, low-fat, or "lite."

Blue is somewhat taboo for foods, as many blue things in nature are poisonous when eaten. Film director and connoisseur of the macabre, Alfred Hitchcock was known for hosting dinner parties at which the food served would be the wrong colors. Many guests, even knowing that the color was only a harmless food dye, couldn't bring themselves to eat blue mashed potatoes.

TRADITIONS OF BLUE

Among the many traditions that began in the Royal Navy is the appetite for faded blue. Naval uniforms were dyed with indigo; ultimately, a sailor's length of service could be read by how faded his uniform had become. Young recruits didn't want to appear inexperienced, and would scrub their uniforms to quickly make them paler blue. Eventually, a color-fast dye was introduced.

NOT EVERY WOMAN CAN WEAR RED

Red Parfum and Eau de Toilette from the Geoffrey Beene Fragrance Collection.

Red is a powerful color with a host of complicated and contradictory associations. The slogan for this ad, created for Geoffrey Beene by Henry Wolf Productions, is an expression from the fashion industry about the color's tendency to overpower the wearer; the ad itself evokes much of the riveting, sexy mystique of red without defining it too precisely.

PROJECT   **GEOFFREY BEENE PERFUME**
DESIGNER   **HENRY WOLF PRODUCTIONS**

■□■ Because they are aimed at an audience of people new to the voting process and perhaps even the country, these brochures announcing and explaining municipal elections to Spanish-speaking New Yorkers feature a traditional look, including stars, stripes, and bunting.

DESIGN FIRM   **DESIGNATION INC.**
DESIGNER   **MIKE QUON**

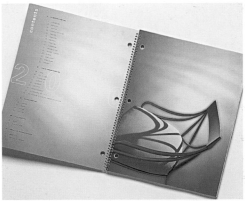

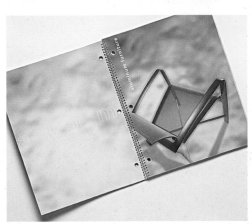

■ ■ ■ Blue, the shade of the sky and the sea, is thought to evoke a soothing atmosphere that calms the spirit. This belief is evident in the Brown Jordan 2000 brochure, a brochure that showcases the furniture-maker's outdoor patio line—quite the opposite of boardroom furniture. Because the furniture is used primarily for leisure activities, designer Jane Kobayshi created the brochure around a palette including restful shades of pastel blue, refreshing, watery hues of blue green, and the rich greens of healthy vegetation. To visually link the palette with the environment, many of the landscape photos echo the colors found in Kobayshi's section openers.

PROJECT	BROWN JORDAN 2000 BROCHURE
DESIGN FIRM	5D STUDIO
ART DIRECTOR/ DESIGNER	JANE KOBAYSHI
PHOTOGRAPHER	SATUSHI
COPYWRITER	RICHARD PRINIER
PRINTER	GEORGE RICE & SONS
CLIENT	BROWN JORDAN

WARNING: MAY BURN OPPONENT

nike

AFTERBURNER FLIGHT

TYPE // AIR AFTERBURNER Flight
DESIGNER // Dr. Jimmy Rockett
WEIGHT // Extremely light
DIMENSIONS // Fit to foot
FOOTLOCKER EXCLUSIVITY // Series 1
PRIMARY FUNCTION // Flexible, lightweight footwear designed to beat your man to a spot
AIR PACK // Large-volume visible Air-Sole unit, super-sculpted midsoles, upper flex zones
MATERIALS OF CONSTRUCTION // UPPER: Combination full-grain floater and synthetic leathers, integrated hidden
eyestay lacing system, TPU reinforced lace locks; MIDSOLE: Lightweight Phylon, large-volume visible Air-Sole
unit; OUTSOLE: Solid rubber Optimal Motion forefoot flex gloves, exposed TPU midfoot shank plate, herringbone
traction pods
INERTIAL GUIDANCE SYSTEM // Enhanced traction focus
MANEUVERABILITY // Omnidirectional responsiveness via encapsulated, large-volume visible Air-Sole unit
PENETRATION CAPABILITY // Athlete propulsion systems

Yellow signals caution and warning; when combined with red, they communicate danger and hazards ahead. Together, the color palette "provokes self-protective and self-interested reactions in the reader. It motivates the reader to scrutinize the message," said Joshua Berger of Plazm Media. When the design studio was asked to create a brand identity for Air Afterburner, a high-profile, top performance line of footwear from Nike, the team chose yellow and red were the colors chosen by the team because of these associations, which parallel the shoes' profile—dangerous to all those except the wearer. "Few can resist the necessity to learn how a product can do them harm. In the case of Afterburner, the reward is a lighthearted marketing message that conceals the necessary product pitch to motivate the final sale," added Berger. The primary mark was spunoff into a series of promotional materials including a 12-foot (3.7 m) window display, wall plaques, and shelf strips.

PROJECT   NIKE AIR AFTERBURNER BRAND IDENTITY
DESIGN FIRM   PLAZM MEDIA
ART DIRECTORS   JOSHUA BERGER, NIKO COURTELIS,
                  PETE MCCRACKEN
DESIGNERS   JOSHUA BERGER, PETE MCCRACKEN
PHOTOGRAPHY   RAPHAEL ASTORGA
COPYWRITER   BARTON CORLEY
CLIENT   NIKE

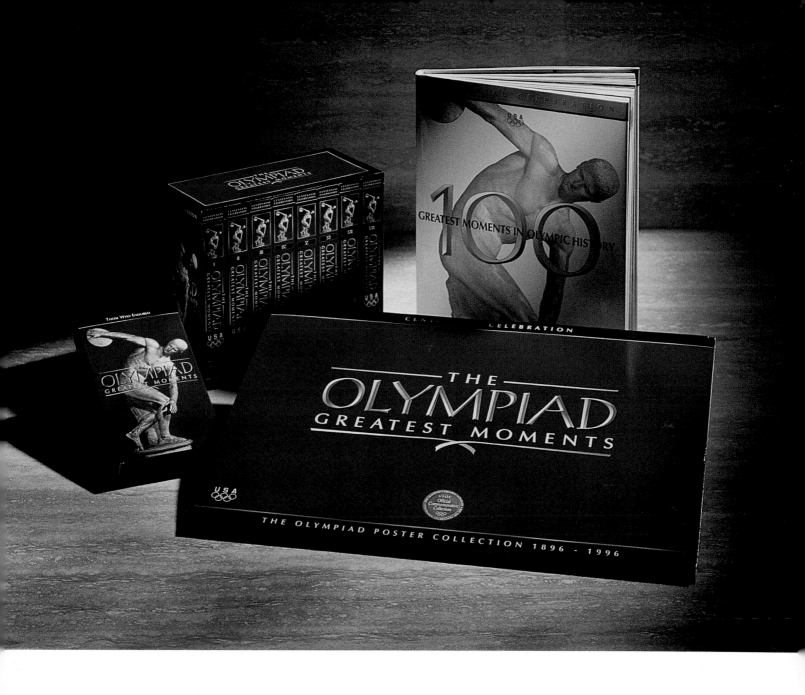

30Sixty Design used a red and gold color scheme—almost universally connected with royalty and pageantry—for materials commemorating the centennial of the modern Olympic games.

PROJECT   **OLYMPIAD GREATEST MOMENTS PACKAGING**
DESIGN FIRM   **30SIXTY DESIGN**

■ Against a gray and gritty urban backdrop, the high visibility of yellow is all the more evident. Using the client's signature color, a warm yellow-gold, to great advantage, the Supon Design Group's banners for a traveling exhibit of the Smithsonian Institute immediately catches the eye of passersby long before the text can be read clearly.

PROJECT   SMITHSONIAN INSTITUTE BANNERS
DESIGN FIRM   SUPON DESIGN GROUP

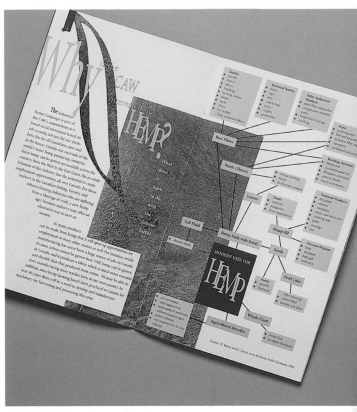

Canadian designer James Peters chose green—and varying shades of green—for this brochure to convey vitality, rebirth, and optimism. "It is a color related to all things that are new, fresh, pleasing, and adventurous," said Peters. "The color calls up associations of spring and new vegetable life. Green is also associated with youth and enterprise." Working with green sometimes proved problematic, much like dressing in this shade; it looks good on the hanger, but doesn't always flatter every individual. Peters decided not to use any color that would weaken the effect of the green or overpower it. "Bright red would have overwhelmed the green by asserting itself in contrast too strongly. An opposite effect would have been produced by the use of grays and blues, which would have dragged down the optimism of the green," he explained. "On the other hand, used in isolation, green can become monotonous."

To avoid these problems, Peters incorporated several shades of green into the design for variety. The secondary palette—a dull red, orange, mauve, and beige—was chosen to be subordinate to the green. In total, the effect was regarded as "positive, pleasing, and even elegant in Canada," added Peters, noting that green is a popular shade in spring and summer fashions in the country.

PROJECT   **SMOKE THIS BOOK**
DESIGN FIRM   **TERRAPIN GRAPHICS**
ART DIRECTOR/
DESIGNER   **JAMES PETERS**
ILLUSTRATOR   **DANA BOETTGER (COVER PAINTING)**
PHOTOGRAPHER   **HELEN DALEY**
           (WORKERS HEALTH AND SAFETY CENTRE)
COPYWRITER   **CANADIAN AUTO WORKERS**
PRINTER   **JBM RESOURCE NETWORK LTD.**
CLIENT   **CANADIAN AUTO WORKERS**

N O W   Y O U   C A N   B A T H E   I N   I T .

GIORGIO
Beverly Hills

The trademark yellow stripes of Giorgio perfume are
known well enough to allow Mike Salisbury to transpose
them into a bathtub for an ad announcing a new line of
bath products. The white tile and gold fixtures add an
elegant, luxurious touch.

PROJECT   **GIORGIO BATH PRODUCTS AD**
DESIGN FIRM   **MIKE SALISBURY COMMUNICATIONS INC.**

Designed by Stefan Sagmeister, a ghostly image of rock star Lou Reed hovers behind the cobalt blue of this CD cover as if emerging from twilight depths, apropos to the title song, *Set the Twilight Reeling*. The conveyance of deep feeling, mystery, distance, and the blues—musical and emotional—is in keeping with the moody singer/songwriter's image; the inner sleeve of the packaging is a bright yellow that signals the underlying optimism of the music.

PROJECT	LOU REED CD
DESIGN FIRM	SAGMEISTER INC.
ART DIRECTOR	STEFAN SAGMEISTER
DESIGNERS	STEFAN SAGMEISTER, VERONICA OH
ILLUSTRATOR	TONY FITZPATRICK
PHOTOGRAPHER	TIMOTHY GREENFIELD SANDERS, PETE CORNISH
CLIENT	WARNER BROS.

Miriello Grafico signals the purity of this bottled water
by the cool, uncomplicated blue and green of its label.
These colors signify refreshment and relief from heat
and dryness.

PROJECT   **PERLA WATER PACKAGING**
DESIGN FIRM   **MIRIELLO GRAFICO, INC.**

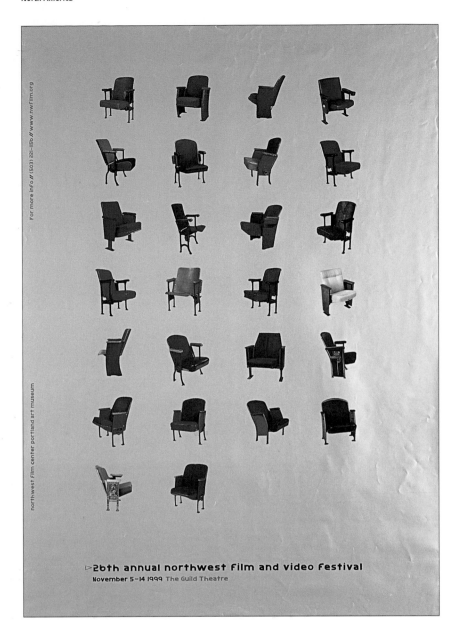

Movies are shown on the "silver screen" and Hollywood is known as "Tinsel Town," so designers chose silver as the background for photographic essay on theater seats in this poster that celebrates the history of the cinema. "Shiny metallic colors are frequently associated with the cinema. Flash, the play of light, glamour, and glitz are all associated with the entertainment industry," said Joshua Berger, art director and designer on the project.

PROJECT	26TH ANNUAL NORTHWEST FILM AND VIDEO FESTIVAL POSTER
DESIGN FIRM	PLAZM MEDIA
ART DIRECTORS	JOSHUA BERGER, NIKO COURTELIS, PETE MCCRACKEN
DESIGNERS	JOSHUA BERGER, JON STEINHORST, WEST YOUSSI, GUS NIKLOS
PHOTOGRAPHY	MARK EBSEN
CLIENT	NORTHWEST FILM CENTER

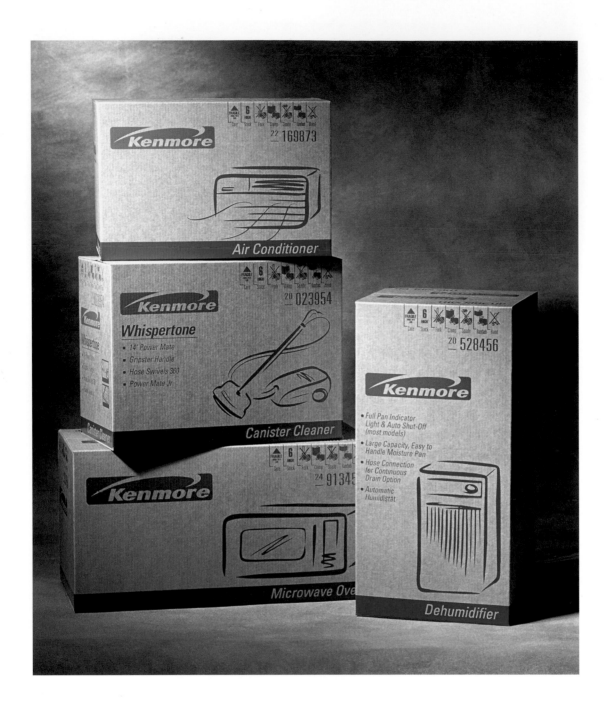

The spare graphic imagery chosen by Source Inc. for Kenmore allows the cartons' color and texture to reinforce the no-nonsense image of Kenmore, as well as the sturdiness and durability associated with the brand.

PROJECT   **KENMORE PACKAGING**
DESIGN FIRM   **SOURCEINC.**

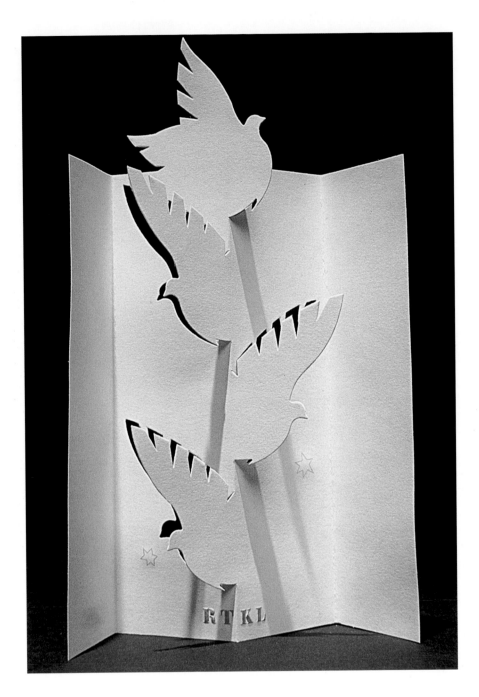

☐ A holiday card created and sent out by RTKL Associates
uses white paper to reinforce an elegant die-cut image
of the dove of peace, implying as well the white of a
snowy winter season.

PROJECT   **HOLIDAY GREETING CARD**
DESIGN FIRM   **RTKL ASSOCIATES**

GREY FLANNEL suits any man

■ To advertise Geoffrey Beene's Grey Flannel cologne for men, Henry Wolf Productions turned more than one cliché on its head. In the 1950s, The Man in the Grey Flannel Suit was emblematic of soulless corporate conformity. By focusing on the pebbly texture of the fabric, the designer conveys richness and complexity, implying that there is more to grey flannel than meets the eye; a grey flannel suit (and Beene's eponymous cologne) resonate with adulthood, power, sophistication, and masculinity.

PROJECT   GEOFFREY BEENE GREY FLANNEL ADVERTISING
DESIGNER   HENRY WOLF PRODUCTIONS

INTO ANOTHER LIGHT

■■ Sonny Sharrock died before this CD was released. His last recording was titled *Into Another Light*, so it was only fitting that the CD jacket reflect the passing of Sharrock with black, the color of death and mourning in the U.S. and most of Western civilization. Designers carried the theme through to the actual CD—using a dark purple color at its outer most edges, which fades and gets lighter toward the center of the CD—symbolic of moving into another light or afterlife.

PROJECT	SONNY SHARROCK CD
DESIGN FIRM	SAGMEISTER INC.
ART DIRECTOR	STEFAN SAGMEISTER
DESIGNERS	STEFAN SAGMEISTER, VERONICA OH
PHOTOGRAPHER	ADAM FUSS
PRINTER	IVY HILL
CLIENT	ENEMY RECORDS

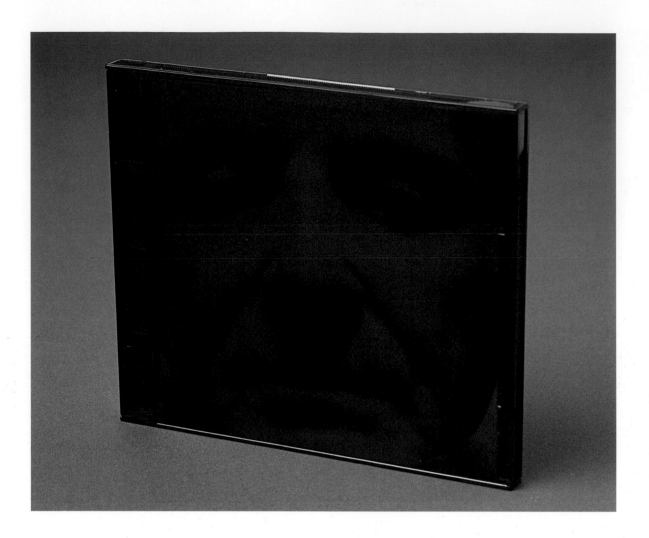

■ ■ Red is symbolic of many things in the U.S. from patriotism and sex appeal to festive celebrations such as Christmas and Valentine's Day, but it has its dark side, too, as seen in the CD jacket design for H.P. Zinger's *Mountains of Madness*. Madness is the theme of the album with lyrics that speak of schizophrenia and how the city can make you crazy. To give madness a visual equivalent, Stefan Sagmeister asked photographer Tom Schierlitz to photograph an old man in a calm and frantic pose. Sagmeister had the calm image printed in green and the frantic image overprinted in red on the CD insert. When the insert is slid into a red-tinted plastic jewel case, the green image turns black, leaving only the man's calm exterior—the red image—visible. When the insert is removed from the case, the manic personality hidden behind the calm façade becomes readily apparent. Photographic pages in the insert get the same treatment, which create the very eerie feeling that madness lurks just beneath the surface.

PROJECT   **H.P. ZINGER *MOUNTAINS OF MADNESS* CD**
DESIGN FIRM   **SAGMEISTER INC.**
ART DIRECTION   **STEFAN SAGMEISTER**
DESIGNERS   **STEFAN SAGMEISTER, VERONICA OH**
PHOTOGRAPHER   **TOM SCHIERLITZ**
CLIENT   **ENERGY RECORDS**

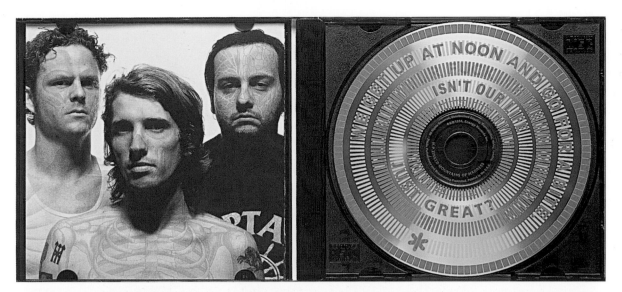

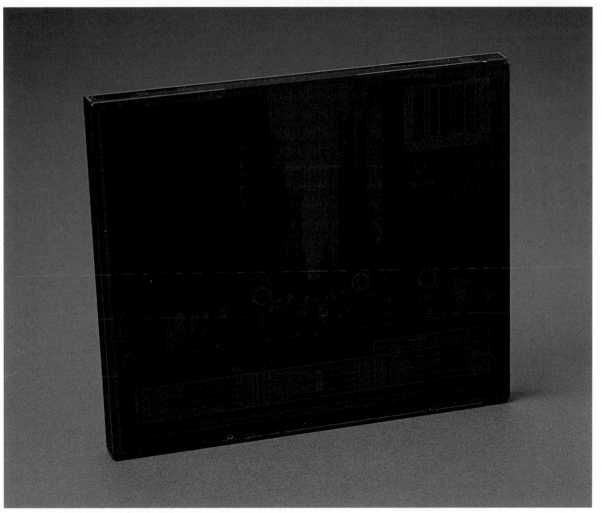

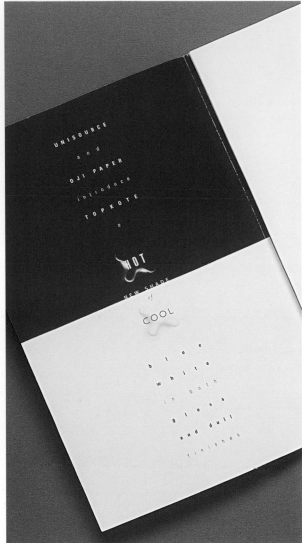

When Oji Paper introduced a new bright blue-white shade of Topkote Gloss and Dull papers, Unisource, a paper merchant, asked 5D Studio to introduce the new product. "We used Unisource red on the cover to tie into the client's corporate look and played with the concept/announcement 'red alert,'" said Jane Kobayshi. Using the theme red alert, a phrase meaning a heightened state of awareness, as the attention-getter, once inside the brochure, the design team employed a stark white palette. They addressed the concept of white space and answer the question, "What makes a color white?" while dropping occasional spots of red into the mix to continue the original theme.

PROJECT   OJI PAPER TOPKOTE BROCHURE
DESIGN FIRM 5D STUDIO
ART DIRECTOR JANE KOBAYSHI
DESIGNER   ANNE COATES
COPYWRITER   ANNE COATES AND VARIOUS
PRINTER   INSYNC MEDIA
CLIENT   UNISOURCE

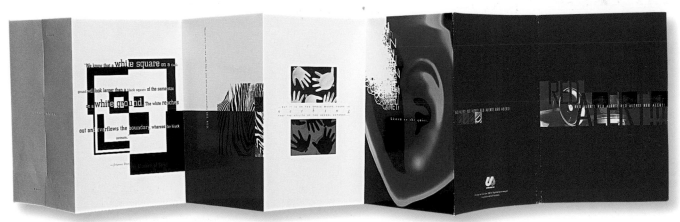

The text within the image (calligraphy):

Time and trouble will tame a young man, but a woman is untamable by any earthly force. A tribute to Gennie and Mabel and Ruth, Peggy, Rosie and the coach and Emma Horton and Lois Jarrett & the women of the novels of Larry McMurtry

TEXAS DESIGNERS ON TEXAS WRITERS

A devil in a pink dress—a pink wedding dress—is the
highlight of this limited edition poster for an AIGA
Houston event Texas Designers on Texas Writers. Pink, a

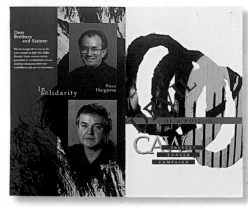

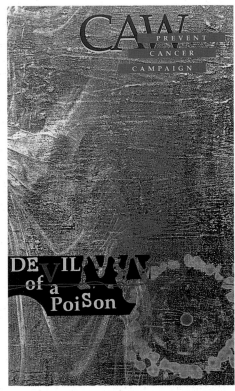

32 · 33

In this brochure, created as part of a preventative cancer campaign in Canada, cancer is equated with the devil and poison—all symbolically represented in the color red, supplemented by brown and a dirty shade of gold. Red, associated with blood and internal organs, was a relatively easy color choice for the designer. The secondary color palette was more subjective. In choosing the brown and dull shade of gold, designer James Peters assumed people would respond to the shades as he did—sensing a relation to disease and corruption. "Colors that are produced by a mix of many primary colors are not in a sense pure like red, yellow, and blue. Instead, there is always the implication of murkiness in mixed colors, of something that is unsettling, brooding," Peters said. "This effect is enhanced if black is

also one of the components of the mixed color, as it is in the case of the brown and dirty gold used in the booklet."

Peters eliminated any colors that would conflict with the palette. "Too much blue would have set up all kinds of unpleasant oppositions in the design and color scheme of the booklet," he explained.

To reinforce his color choices, Peters chose imagery in keeping with the theme—decayed walls and graveyards—to convey the grim purpose of the booklet without repulsing readers. Peters' sensitivity to the topic has paid-off. The booklet has been reprinted three times and is being translated into French for added distribution.

PROJECT	DEVIL OF A POISON BROCHURE
DESIGN FIRM	TERRAPIN GRAPHICS
ART DIRECTOR/	
DESIGNER	JAMES PETERS
ILLUSTRATOR	DANA BOETTGER (COVER PAINTING)
PHOTOGRAPHER	HELEN DALEY (WORKERS HEALTH AND SAFETY CENTRE)
COPYWRITER	CANADIAN AUTO WORKERS
PRINTER	JBM RESOURCE NETWORK LTD.
CLIENT	CANADIAN AUTO WORKERS

about us

what's on

families

kids

funstuff

talkback

f family

1999 This is television of the family, for the family, and by the family.

Check it Out!

fan poL

Angels in the Endzone
Christopher Lloyd stars as Al the Angel in this Disney Comedy.

Sat., Nov. 20 at 8:00 pm (ET/PT)

Quicklinks!

con tests

Family Power.
Turn it on!

The Family Channel provided Yfactor Inc. with limited color schemes developed for television, which the design firm modified for use on the television network's Web site. Ask kids in Canada and the U.S. what their favorite color is and the answer is likely to be blue. With that in mind, Yfactor created a kid-friendly Internet venue with lots of blue and other bright colors to differentiate the contents of the site. The color palette is youthful, eye-catching, and exciting; geared to target kids and families with kids in North America.

PROJECT THE FAMILY CHANNEL WEB SITE
DESIGN FIRM YFACTOR, INC.
ART DIRECTOR ANYA COLUSSI
DESIGNER JOHN JUNG
CLIENT THE FAMILY CHANNEL

■ An often-maligned color choice, orange is coming into its own. Designer Susan Lee chose orange to represent the corporate identity of her firm, named Orange, to align with the future direction of color trends. Orange conveys "contemporary design, bordering edgy street fashion. It's a fresh, upbeat color for the new millennium. Combined with the tech-color silver, orange reflects a retro reinvention of the past with the industrial sensibilities of traffic/danger signs. All of these color trends have had an impact on North American product and graphic design, which is now catching up with Europe where designers have been integrating orange for much longer," said Lee.

PROJECT	ORANGE CORPORATE BROCHURE
DESIGN FIRM	ORANGE
ART DIRECTOR/	
DESIGNER	SUSAN LEE
PHOTOGRAPHER	VERVE PHOTOGRAPHICS
COPYWRITERS	JACQUIE VERKLEY, SUT FITTERMAN, SUSAN LEE
PRINTER	METROPOLITAN FINE PRINTERS
CLIENT	ORANGE INFORMATION DESIGN OFFICE

Latin America

The use and significance of color in Latin America follows the European model, primarily as practiced in Spain and other predominantly Catholic countries. Underlying this is the pre-Columbian history of the region.

The church and the social order imposed by Spain and Portugal in the 16th and 17th centuries took root to varying degrees in each region of Latin America, which shows in its architecture; the decoration of chapels and the portrayal of saints and biblical figures took on a distinctive local flavor, incorporating elements of pre-Colombian art and worship.

Latin Americans have ambivalent feelings about their pre-Colombian past, unsure whether to relegate it to history or proudly embrace it. Many native peoples have continuing folk art traditions, but their traditional ways are as alien and exotic to most urban Latin Americans as something from the other side of the world. On the other hand, Latin Americans avidly consume products from Europe and the United States, and are familiar with brand names from each. Consumer items, along with films and television programs, often arrive with no changes besides translation.

One caution: Be aware of lingering animosities between neighboring countries and avoid using or invoking the flag or national colors from a historic rival. Of the many pre-Colombian societies that once flourished, the Mayan, Aztec, and Inca civilizations had the most lasting impact on post-Colonial Latin America, and color significance attributable to them is discussed in the following sections. Much of the discussion of Western Civilization on pages 62-65 is relevant to Latin America as well.

Mexico

Mexico honors its vivid history and culture with everyday use of brilliant hues.

The Mexican flag is red, white, and green, with the national symbol (eagle attacking snake) in the center section. These national colors are used to identify the country in a variety of imagery.

The aesthetic heritage of Mexico includes the influence of the Olmec, Mayan, and Aztec civilizations combined with those of Spain, the Caribbean, and to a lesser degree France and the Philippines. Mexico was the centerpiece of Spanish colonialism in the New World. Mexican Indians (nativos) maintain a link to their past through folk art, and the country as a whole is more connected to its pre-Columbian past than many other Latin American nations. In contrast to the somber look of their Spanish conquerors, Mexican culture developed a tradition of vivid decoration and colorful festivals. Everyday objects often sport brilliant colors. The traditional serape (poncho) worn by the peasantry typically has broad alternating stripes of green, red, and yellow. Like grown-up versions of the paper umbrellas that adorn exotic drinks, parasols sold on the streets of Mexico City are embellished with swirls of pink, orange, and green.

The geography, climate, and local materials, combined with the predilection of the Spanish colonists, resulted in the Mediterranean/North African look of traditional Mexican architecture. Whitewashed adobe and terra cotta roof tiles are basic, and there is the Moorish influence of the Alhambra in Spain. The decorative tilework that Mexico is known for—geometric, highly stylized floral shapes, usually blue on white—and that is now identified with its former possession, California, is descended directly from the Islamic patterned tiles that the Moors introduced to Spain during their occupation. Through its layers of architecture, Mexico City mirrors the history of the country: Aztec temples are buried underneath 17th century Spanish colonial churches and public buildings, which have been decorated with 20th century murals. One section of the city, constructed in the 1850s, deliberately resembles Paris; while the modern architecture of Luis Barragan, constructed in the 1940s and 1950s, is spare, minimalist and painted in florid colors—the hot pinks and oranges of bougainvillea blossoms.

Aztec theology revolved around the duality of existence; day and night, light and dark, male and female, reflected in the pairing of contrasting colors (not unlike the Buddhist yin-yang). Aztec handweaving combines about 200 different colors, primarily for decorative purposes and without symbolic significance. Characteristic Aztec colors included deep reds, clay brown, straw and lemon yellow, turquoise, emerald green, gray, and black. Points of the Aztec compass were color-coded: east was gold; west was turquoise and jade green; south was white; north was red.

A favorite in religious and secular decor, red (here as in all of Latin America) is readily available as a dye from the cochineal bug. In most Indian mythology, red is the color of the sun, although gold is often used to portray it.

The Aztec god who held up the sky was named Kan, which is also the Aztec word for yellow. In Mexican folk art, yellow is a popular background color.

Dark blue as well as black is worn for mourning, though these colors are not exclusive to funeral attire. One Aztec god was born carrying a blue spear and shield, and had his arms and legs painted blue.

The meanings of green are linked with vegetation. Mayan tombs were painted jade green, perhaps to symbolize the earth reclaiming the dead—just as the jungle could quickly obscure the manmade.

Gold is used as a display of wealth. Both the Mayans and the Aztecs used gold extensively and extravagantly. Starting with the Spanish Colonial period, most gold objects were made for and are only seen in churches.

Black is the color of death, mourning, priestly robes, and the somber clothing of the Castillian aristocracy that once ruled Mexico. As elsewhere in Western society, black clothing demands respect.

Both in contrast to the aristocratic connotations of black and the often intense heat and sunshine, white is the traditional color for peasant daily wear. Otherwise, white also signifies purity and cleanliness.

The Spanish established silver mines soon after their conquest of the Aztec empire, which had used the metal extensively, and Mexico became a chief supplier of silver. Finely crafted silverwork—both everyday items and jewelry—became, and remains, a hallmark of Mexico.

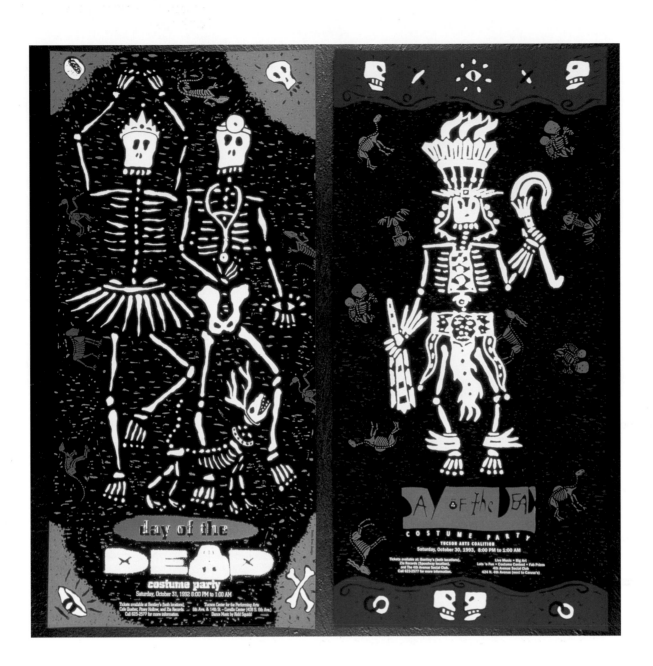

■■ Red and black, the customary colors of death and the apocalypse, are used for a Boelts Bros. invitation to a costume party celebrating the Mexican Day of the Dead festival. Traditionally celebrated at the beginning of November, the holiday's customs include all-night picnicking in the cemetery in which one's ancestors are buried.

PROJECT   "DAY OF THE DEAD" INVITATION
DESIGN FIRM   BOELTS BROS.

■ ■ ■ For a tourist brochure promoting the border town of
Tijuana, Scott Mires Design of San Diego, California,
used a hot, festive palette drawn from the local landscape and the reputation of the city as an exotic, exciting, and adventurous destination.

PROJECT   TIJUANA TOURISM BROCHURE
DESIGN FIRM   MIRES DESIGN
DESIGNER   SCOTT MIRES

Designers were asked to create a regional stamp that reflected the country of origin and flavor profile of an organic coffee grown in Mexico. To accomplish this goal, designers referenced images and styles from Mexico to replicate the look and feel of the country's folk art. Inspiration came from the handmade papers used in many native crafts. They used these substrates as the basis for the textured, tan background color of the stamp, which perfectly symbolized the natural organic quality of the coffee. They used red to highlight the shade-grown message (shade-grown coffee has minimal impact on the environment) and green to convey the organic quality of the coffee. Coincidentally, red and green are also the primary colors of the Mexican flag.

The border is inspired by the bold patterns found on many Mexican ceramic products, while the bird and coffee cherry icons again were taken from the native handicrafts that depict jungle parrots and parakeets found in Chipas, Mexico, the region where the coffee is grown. According to Starbucks, they represent the partnership between man and nature and symbolize environmentally sustainable agriculture.

PROJECT	STARBUCKS COFFEE SHADE GROWN MEXICO LOGO
DESIGN FIRM	STARBUCKS DESIGN GROUP
ART DIRECTOR	MICHAEL CORY
DESIGNER	KLINDT PARKER
ILLUSTRATOR	MARTINA WITTE
CLIENT	STARBUCKS COFFEE COMPANY

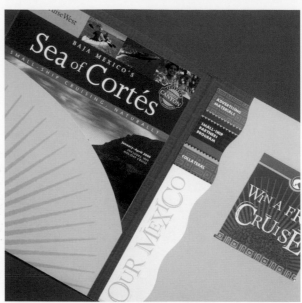

■ ■ ■ Belyea created this multi-piece package to encourage travel agents to sell Cruise West's newest cruise destination. The pieces are distinctive for the warm color palette that is indigenous to Mexico, including yellow, orange, and khaki—reflecting the sun and terra cotta tiles of Mexico—plus deep blues and teals signifying the water attractions. Aztec graphics are used on the folder and as a border on the poster, where a map of the region is rendered in teal and coppery hues in a pattern like that of traditional Mexican mosaic tiles.

PROJECT	CRUISE WEST MEXICO PROMOTIONAL MATERIALS
DESIGN FIRM	BELYEA
ART DIRECTOR	PATRICIA BELYEA
DESIGNER	RON LARS HANSEN
COPYWRITER	LIZ HOLLAND
PRINTER	COLOR GRAPHICS

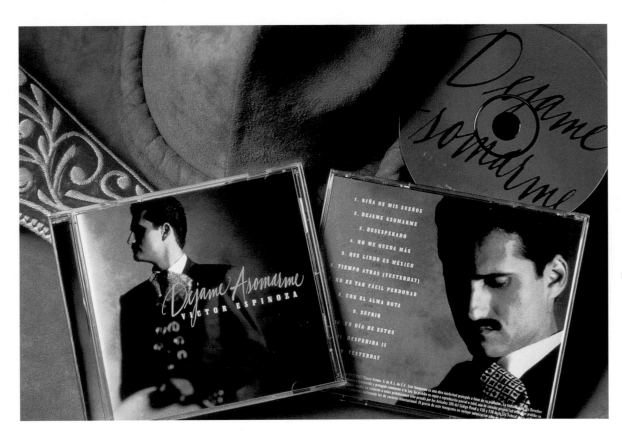

42 · 43

■ To communicate the romantic qualities of Victor Espinoza's music in the CD packaging, Mires Design opted for an earthy, sepia-toned photograph of an authentically costumed singer to reinforce the traditional nature of Mexican mariachi music. The CD was targeted to consumers in Mexico.

PROJECT	VICTOR ESPINOZA *DEJAME ASOMARME* CD
DESIGN FIRM	MIRES DESIGN, INC.
ART DIRECTOR	JOHN BALL
DESIGNER	MIGUEL PEREZ
PHOTOGRAPHER	CHRIS WIMPEY
PRINTER	RUSH PRESS
CLIENT	VICTOR ESPINOZA

Starbucks Coffee Company designer Joe Cachero used a tan background to highlight the company's Organic Costa Rica stamp because the color is perceived by many to be more environmental than slick white. Located at the southern tip of Mexico, Costa Rica shares its color traditions with Mexico, the Caribbean, and South America, and is a country with a rich agricultural heritage including bananas, sugarcane, rice, plantains, and coffee. The icon used in this design represents the people and coffee of Costa Rica; the border pattern is indigenous to the region.

PROJECT   STARBUCKS COFFEE ORGANIC
                 COSTA RICA STAMP
DESIGN FIRM   STARBUCKS DESIGN GROUP
DESIGNER   JOE CACHERO
CLIENT   STARBUCKS COFFEE COMPANY

To generate the feeling of a premium, handpicked, coffee grown without use of pesticides, designers created a simple tree illustration and printed it in one color on French Durotone Packing Brown Wrap paper stock. Equally as notable as the choice of the logo's earthy brown palette is the illustration itself. Because the coffee is handpicked, the leaves of the tree, known as a Starbucks "grow icon," are significant and represent the people of Costa Rica.

PROJECT	STARBUCKS COFFEE ORGANIC COSTA RICA STAMP
DESIGN FIRM	STARBUCKS DESIGN GROUP
ART DIRECTOR	JOE CACHERO
DESIGNER/ ILLUSTRATOR	MARK MCGINNIS
CLIENT	STARBUCKS COFFEE COMPANY

An earth-friendly color palette of natural tan, brown, and orange reinforce Costa Rica Natural's reputation as an environmentally conscientious company while enhancing recognition for its product, a natural fiber paper. The warm color palette also plays to the company's Cigar Paper and is evocative of the hues found in the tobacco-growing region of Costa Rica. "This color palette is richly natural, like vegetable dyes, and suggests a handmade process," said Sonia Greteman. It also "suggests a return to a more natural environment and reinforces the recycled nature of the coffee, banner, and cigar fibers. No artificial colors, metallic, or fluorescent inks were used."

PROJECT	COSTA RICA NATURAL BUSINESS CARD AND PACKAGING
DESIGN FIRM	GRETEMAN GROUP
ART DIRECTOR	SONIA GRETEMAN
DESIGNER	JAMES STRANGE
CLIENT	COSTA RICA NATURAL

The Caribbean

Bahamas, Cuba, Jamaica, Haiti, Dominican Republic, Puerto Rico, Lesser Antilles

Puerto Rico's and Cuba's flags are like variations of the American Stars and Stripes, both in design and color scheme. Jamaica and Bermuda both contain black, which is said to symbolize the burdens the people have suffered under.

Brilliant flowering plants against the backdrop of lush, deep green vegetation is a keynote in a Caribbean color scheme, which echoes the region's brilliantly hued plant and sea life. The tradition of painting houses and buildings in bright colors has antecedents in both Latin America and Africa. Carnivals and funerals are both wildly colorful events; daily life isn't exactly monochromatic.

As word of Spain's 15th and 16th century forays into the New World spread, every European nation with a fleet laid claim to one or another Caribbean island, setting off a centuries-long game of musical colonies; some islands changed hands every decade or so. By the time the Caribbean islands began to gain independence, the indigenous inhabitants were long gone, and the region's population consisted of the descendants of African slaves and Europeans who preferred the islands' climate and lifestyle to those of the Old World.

Today, these islands carry a legacy of multicultural influences, starting with the Spanish. The pan-African and Rastafarian colors of red, yellow, and green are popular and commonly used even by those outside the Rastafarians (these are the colors of the Jamaican flag) as a show of affiliation with the society's African roots. The primary cultural influence will be that of the last or the longest-lasting colonizer of the island; in some cases, a larger world power still holds the deed. Britain still administers Anguilla, Bermuda (not technically in the Caribbean), the British Virgin Islands, the Caymans, Montserrat, and the Turks and Caicos. British influence is also strong in Barbados (dubbed "Little England" by neighboring islands), the Bahamas, Jamaica, St. Kitts and Nevis, St. Vincent, Trinidad and Tobago. France held Haiti for decades, and Martinique and Guadeloupe are still French possessions. Aruba and the Netherlands Antilles are all that Holland retains of its Caribbean colonial adventure. Puerto Rico, and the U.S. Virgin Islands are possessions of the United States. St. Lucia and Dominica were each held by Britain and France at one time or another.

Red plays a significant role in the Caribbean landscape. The Bahamas, for instance, is known for its distinctive red poinsettias. Oleander, an evergreen shrub that blossoms with pink, red, or white flowers, is common in Bermuda and often used as hedgerows. And in Antigua and Barbuda, the red-billed tropic bird is ubiquitous.

Green symbolizes the lush vegetation of the Caribbean islands—as well as some of the local inhabitants. Puerto Rico's El Yunque National Forest boasts 240 types of trees and giant ferns, not to mention the bright-green tree frog, the coquí, which is something of a Puerto Rican mascot.

Yellow, along with red and green, is one of the pan-African and Rastafarian colors and can be found in Jamaica's flag. Yellow also holds a place of honor in the Bahamas, where the yellow elder is the national flower. For a bird's-eye view of the Caribbean color scheme, check out Aruba's little yellow-bellied barika geel bird. In Antigua and Barbuda, yellow-crowned night herons are a common sight.

On the streets of Puerto Rico's Old San Juan you'll notice the preponderance of soft pastel colors, not the least of which are varying shades of pink, on many of the buildings.

Blue inevitably means water in the Caribbean. The Bahamas Platform's shallow waters are spectacular shades of turquoise and ultramarine. In Antigua, blue is also for the birds, including the great blue heron, which can be found in the Potworks Dam in the spring.

It's not surprising that a clean, cool color such as white would be popular in the Caribbean. The roofs of houses in Bermuda are typically white and furrowed to facilitate collecting water. And white figures into local tourist trade: jewelry featuring the white seagoing long-tail is a local favorite. Bahamian police wear starched white uniforms.

The trupiaal, with bright orange features, is the most common bird in Aruba. A pale shade of orange, bordering on peach, is plentiful and is the color of coral.

Black is inextricably linked with pirate lore from this region. Pirates were known to wear black eye-patches and black hats. The Jolly Roger, the flag of pirate ships, is black and is known as Captain Death among pirates.

Like black, gold and silver had significant meaning that can be traced back to the days when pirates sailed their ships in and out of the many coves and inlets of the Caribbean islands. A pirate's booty often consisted of doubloons and "pieces of eight," heavy silver and gold coins. Pirates depicted in the movies, and those chronicled in history, were also known to sport gold earrings.

Golden brown and amber hues are often associates with rum, a distilled alcoholic beverage made from molasses in the Caribbean.

John Sayles employed a vivid palette of magenta, lime green, and teal to convey the tropical allure of a four-day Caribbean getaway to the Virgin Islands, a trip sponsored by Galileo International, a travel management company. Sayles hand-rendered a patterned design to capture the exotic feel of the islands and used lively photographs of the sights. Raffia and golden bead binding finish off the piece, adding a natural touch as well as the glamour inherent in this popular tourist locale.

PROJECT	VIRGIN ISLANDS GETAWAY INVITATION
DESIGN FIRM	SAYLES GRAPHIC DESIGN
ART DIRECTOR/	
DESIGNER/	
ILLUSTRATOR	JOHN SAYLES
COPYWRITER	WENDY LYONS
CLIENT	GALILEO INTERNATIONAL

Miriello Grafico's Chris Keeney created the color palette for this vitamin packaging from the colors he found in the Caribbean landscape and surrounding areas, including South America. The vitamins are manufactured in Aruba and are sold throughout South America and eventually will be sold in North America as well. The palette employs a rusty brown, representing the color of the soil; a muted blue, depicting the sky, water, and plant-life; a rich green drawn from the abundant vegetation; and a pale straw color found in the rocks and even the walls of older architectural dwellings.

PROJECT   VISSER VITAMIN LABELS
DESIGN FIRM   MIRIELLO GRAFICO, INC.
DESIGNER   CHRIS KEENEY
CLIENT   DR. RICHARD VISSER

As is designer Chris Keeney's practice, when faced with developing a color palette and color combinations for twelve different baseball caps, he turned to nature and the local environs for inspiration. Spirit is headquartered in the Caribbean, specifically Aruba, but the hats Keeney was asked to design would be sold throughout South America as well. During an extensive tour of Latin America, including Mexico, Yucatan, Guatemala, and Peru, he took a myriad of photos depicting the local landscape and noted that the Spirit store is surrounded by high and low desert areas contrasting with lush tropical forests. With so much local color to choose from, he had his palette.

Back at the studio, he reviewed his photos and chose color combinations that appear naturally together and compliment one another in nature. Working with these earth tones, he colored twelve hats in various hues found in lichens, cactus, agave, and the sky. The effect is striking, particularly when one compares the finished hat colors against the original landscape photos that provided the inspiration.

PROJECT	SPIRIT BASEBALL CAPS
DESIGN FIRM	MIRIELLO GRAFICO, INC.
DESIGNER	CHRIS KEENEY
CLIENT	SPIRIT

South America

Color conventions and significance in South America were imported from Europe, primarily Spain, and mixed with African and indigenous cultures; this aesthetic Creole prevails throughout Latin America, where crafts show a blending of Indian and Spanish colonial imagery (textile and pottery designs tend towards a stronger native sensibility).

Beyond the Andes (and the former Inca empire) the meanings of colors have long differed from region to region and tribe to tribe, and have been used for purely decorative reasons. The single truly unifying aspect of color in South America is the frequent and widespread use of red, thanks to the Incas developing vivid and lasting red dyes and paint from various local ingredients.

The Incas and Their Andean Descendants

The Incas, who were in power when the Conquistadors arrived, called gold "blood of the sun" and silver "tears of the moon." Their use of such metals emphasized spiritual and metaphysical qualities.

Lively abstract patterns and warm colors were characteristic of Inca decorative arts. They produced bright reds that have remained remarkably brilliant over time, and used colors taken—literally—from bright Amazonian birds, retaining specific combinations: the yellow and orange of parrots; the blue of macaws; the green and black of ducks. Inca crafts standardized color and pattern, assuring that items' meaning and value was constant throughout the empire.

Contemporary Andean pottery is often a reddish buff or painted black and yellow, featuring decorative figures of cats, human or bird heads and geometric figures incised into the surface. Generally, the more prosaic an item is, the less colorful; conversely, some folk crafts have become more colorful as their usefulness has diminished, and they are increasingly made only for decorative purposes.

Color use by contemporary Andean tribes is meaningful mostly among themselves. Dark, usually black, woolen clothing is fairly constant among those who live in the mountains; the color of hats, capes, and accessories differ. In Bolivia men of the Tarabuco wear red and orange striped ponchos and hats, while Tarabuco women wear small, white sequin-covered headgear. The women of the Salasaca and Saguro of Ecuador wear black shoulder cloths fastened with a silver pin. Otavalo men wear thick blue ponchos over white trousers, while Otavalo women favor heavily embroidered white blouses. In Colombia, Guambiano Indian women wear layers of loose gray-black wool skirts decorated with horizontal bands of color, and accessorize with blue and fuchsia scarves and decoration. Throughout Andean tribes the chumpi, a wide woven belt, is worn as a talisman and at ceremonial occasions for its protective and purifying qualities. Decorated with ancient (probably Inca) patterns and design, no specific color is dictated by tradition, although red is the most popular. Its resemblance to Zulu beadwork in both style and meaning is remarkable.

Argentina

Argentina's aesthetic is linked more to its ties to Europe than to South America.

The pale shade of blue in this flag is no accident. When the flag was being designed, one political group reportedly wanted a bluish-green color and another group favored a whitish blue. Anything but a dark blue, apparently, was desired. The Argentineans call the blue of their flag, the color of the sky in the daytime, *celeste*.

A self-styled anomaly in South America, Argentina maintains closer cultural links to Europe than to the rest of Latin America, and seem slightly removed from its neighbors and its own native heritage. Even its flag, cool blue and white, is unlike that of other South American nations. Many Argentines trace their ancestry not to Spain but to Italy, Germany, and other European countries. The population is also overwhelmingly urban, with only 15 percent of its people living in rural areas and small towns. Buenos Aires is cosmopolitan. Considered quite sophisticated, it is as trend-conscious and up-to-the-minute as any city on earth. Taxis in metropolitan areas are yellow and black. Those who can afford to seem willing to pay extra money for imported items, as much for the cachet as for any perceived higher quality.

Traditions of the gaucho greatly appeal to the average Argentine. These dashing 19th century horsemen are folk legends. Gaucho fashion included colorful scarves and lots of handcrafted silver items such as belt buckles and knives. Trappings of saddlery grew into a tradition of fine leather crafts.

Red has been a favorite color and in continuous use since the pre-Colombian period, owing in part to the vivid colorfast dyes produced in the region. Baskets woven from palm fibers by the Cholo Indians of Colombia resemble terra cotta pottery, and feature intricate geometrical designs.

To the Incas the significance of blue, the color of sky, expanded to include freedom, infinity, and the blessings of the gods. In Central America and along the coasts, the color is closely associated with the ocean and what it means—travel, goals, ambition, vastness, a source of food and occasional danger.

The rarity, pliability, and decorative properties of gold made it an object of desire for both the Inca and the Conquistadors. Ironically, the societies' use of gold paralleled each other in many ways; in both, it was used for religious relics and ceremonial objects, and was tightly held onto by the elite. Mapuche women of southern Chile display their jewelry as a show of their wealth and social standing, comparable to Bedouin women.

White is commonly worn by peasants in the low country and in any warm climate, owing to its light-reflective, cooling quality. Along with purity and other European implications, white also represents the snow of the Andean peaks and implies heights of accomplishment and aspiration.

Bruno / Garrié Faget
Diseño de comunicación visual

Monica Garrié Faget

Tinogasta 3129 2do 8
1417 Buenos Aires
Tel/fax 502 9293

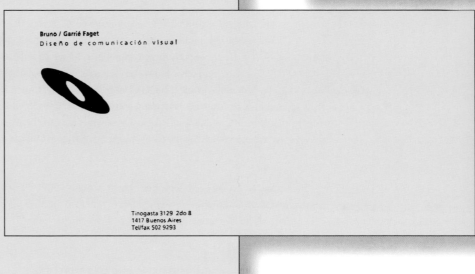

Bruno / Garrié Faget
Diseño de comunicación visual

Tinogasta 3129 2do 8
1417 Buenos Aires
Tel/fax 502 9293

Tinogasta 3129 2do 8
1417 Buenos Aires
Tel/fax 502 9293

Eye-popping yellow is used throughout this design team's letterhead system. It speaks loudly and a letter arriving in this bright yellow envelope is guaranteed to be noticed.

PROJECT	BRUNO / GARRIÉ FAGET CORPORATE IDENTITY
DESIGN FIRM	BRUNO / GARRIÉ FAGET
DESIGNERS	GUSTAVO BRUNO, MÓNICA GARRIÉ FAGET

54 · 55

■■ To introduce Dr. Lemon, a new beverage sold in Argentina, Interbrand Avalos & Brouse relied on a green bottle and a green label, accented with white and orange to convey the refreshing, citrus characteristics of the lemon drink.

PROJECT	DR. LEMON PACKAGING
DESIGN FIRM	INTERBRAND AVALOS & BOURSE
ART DIRECTOR/ DESIGNER	CARLOS AVALOS
ILLUSTRATOR	HORACIO VAZQUEZ
CLIENT	S.A.V.A. GANCIA

■ Deep brown is the color of bock beer and this label in
an equally dark, brownish-burgundy shade reinforces
its rich, robust flavor. The color scheme implies a full-
bodied, full-flavored brew, as far from the pale and
golden ales, and "lite" beers as you can get.

■ Terrazas is a premium priced wine with a global appeal,
however, it is "positioned as a true Argentinean wine
with all the design aesthetics of the region," said Carlos
Avalos. The packaging gets its premium appeal from
the all-black treatment including black wrapping paper
that encases a black bottle while a small gold label and
a golden cord provide an understated accent.

PROJECT	QUILMES BOCK PACKAGING
DESIGN FIRM	INTERBRAND AVALOS & BOURSE
ART DIRECTOR	CARLOS AVALOS
DESIGNER	DIEGO GIACCONE
CLIENT	CERVECERIA Y MALTERIA QUILMES

PROJECT	TERRAZAS WINE PACKAGING
DESIGN FIRM	INTERBRAND AVALOS & BOURSE
ART DIRECTOR/	
DESIGNER	CARLOS AVALOS
ILLUSTRATOR	HORACIO VAZUEZ, HERNÁN CAÑELLAS
CLIENT	BODEGAS CHANDON

56 · 57

Pronto is targeted to a young audience, so its not surprising that designers at Interbrand Avalos & Bourse,
an Argentine design firm, employed illustrations and
type colored with bold, vibrant hues to depict a self-
expressive mood of party-time.

PROJECT	PRONTO SHAKE PACKAGING
DESIGN FIRM	INTERBRAND AVALOS & BOURSE
ART DIRECTOR	CARLOS AVALOS
DESIGNERS	ALLYSON BREIN, DIEGO GIACCONE
ILLUSTRATORS	DANIEL CHASKIELBERG, ALLYSON BREIN, MARIO CANDELAREZZI, HERNAN CAÑELLAS
CLIENT	S.A.V.A. GANCIA

Brazil

The brilliant colors of Amazon flora and fauna inform the Brazilian palette.

The green, white, and blue of Brazil's flag is a distinct from most others in South America.

There are two key elements that distinguish Brazil from the rest of Latin America: The Portuguese, who left a legacy of language and European culture, and the Amazon River. The traditions and the tribes who live along the Amazon and in the surrounding rainforest are vastly different from those who dwell in the Andes, the pampas, or even the jungles of Central America. In many cases there has been virtually no contact between these tribal people and the rest of the country. Still, the brilliant colors of Amazonian flora and fauna inform the Brazilian palette, and the yearly Carnival of Rio de Janeiro reflects the colors of the rainforest.

Red cars are prohibited in Brazil (also in Ecuador) because statistics show that—despite the color's high visibility—red cars are involved in more accidents than cars of any other color. Among the Craho Amazonian tribespeople, corpses are painted red; the best female singer in the village wears a red scarf. Red is a used for cheerful decorative purposes such as Carnival, and has less religious baggage than in much of the rest of the continent.

Purple as the color of mourning is an import from Portugal; it is a sign of respect for God's power over life and death. Brazilian amethyst is a very desirable shade of deep purple.

Emeralds from Colombia flooded the European market when the Conquistadors took over the new continent. Among its purportedly mystical powers, the emerald was said to sweat in the presence of poison, and to cure defective vision. Green is also the color that signifies the rainforest.

Brilliant hues of fiery orange and yellow, found on macaws and other birds as well as floral and fauna in the rainforest, accent the Brazilian palette.

Much of Brazil's color palette comes from nature; the country's exports—hardwoods and Brazil nuts—are shades of warm, golden browns.

The most common color for high-altitude and cold-weather clothing, black also carries implications of Spanish aristocracy and European sophistication. The color of mourning, black is the color worn by widows and priests; it is also the color of choice for many formal occasions, not just funerals.

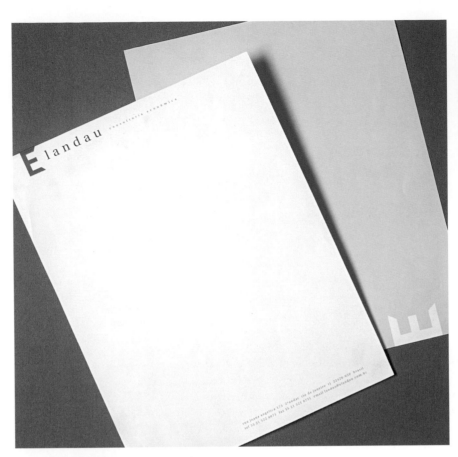

ELandau, a consulting firm specializing in economics, had established itself as a brand name in an industry known for being conservative. ELandau came to Ana Couto Design looking for a makeover that would give the established firm a modern, upbeat image, successfully differentiating it from its competitors. Designers opted to use strong colors, chiefly to reflect the personality of the company's owner, Elena Landau, who is highly regarded and recognized in the Brazilian market economy. Designers chose bold primary colors of red and yellow to reflect ELandau's strong character and vibrancy in the marketplace and carried the color theme through its letterhead, large and small mailing envelopes, cardboard inserts, business cards, and business card jacket/mailers. Each element in the corporate identity system employed this color palette, typically using one color on the front of a piece and juxtaposing the contrasting shade on the reverse.

Prospective clients got their first introduction to the new identity through a direct mail campaign. "The acceptance was immediate and the feedback from clients and prospects was positive, creating awareness for the brand," said Ana Couto.

PROJECT	ELANDAU IDENTITY SYSTEM
DESIGN FIRM	ANA COUTO DESIGN
ART DIRECTOR	ANA COUTO
DESIGNERS	ANA COUTO, NATASCHA BRASIL E DANILO CID
CLIENT	ELANDAU CONSULTORIA ECONÔMICA

■ Inox Tubos manufactures stainless steel tubes. While the Brazilian company is a leader in this category, the market views the product as a commodity item and Inox Tubos wanted to be seen as different. To distinguish the company, Ana Couto Design created a new corporate identity that reflects the firm's agility, reliability, and technology. Designers developed a logotype that is a stylistic representation of how the company makes its products. The choice of metallic blue for the logo not only reflects the color of the client's product—stainless steel—but symbolizes innovation and technology. "The metallic blue brings innovation to the brand without losing its solid and corporate character, essential for the company's image," said Ana Couto. Following the debut of the new logo, Ana Couto Design reported that Inox Tubos's target market began viewing the company as more modern, offering a higher level of technology than its competitors.

PROJECT   INOX TUBOS CORPORATE IDENTITY
DESIGN FIRM   ANA COUTO DESIGN
ART DIRECTOR   ANA COUTO
DESIGNERS   CRISTIANA NOGUEIRA, JAQUELINE FERNANDES,
                 NATASCHA BRASIL
CLIENT   INOX TUBOS

Western Europe

The countries of Europe—east, west, north, and south—share a cohesive set of color conventions and an understanding of colors' significance that far outweighs the differences—and there are plenty—between individual nations.

Generally speaking, the darker the color the more serious, dignified, formal, and sometimes negative its implications; lighter colors take on less formal, more positive meanings. Language reinforces this at every turn; someone might be in a dark mood or have a sunny disposition. A close second consideration is a color's chroma (intensity) or shade (amount of black in the color). This consideration takes the place of surface texture, so important in Asian and African culture.

Marketing to the whole of Europe presents many problems; fortunately color isn't a big one. There are national and regional differences, preferences and traditions of color, but the potential for color-related faux pas pales in comparison to those made possible by the language barrier— Spain's Dye gin or France's Pschitt lemonade drink would be hard to sell in Great Britain. Nevertheless, long before the concept of the European Commonwealth, trade between European countries created familiarity with brand names and a largely borderless marketplace.

While the significance of the colors discussed on the following pages originated in Europe, many of their associations hold true throughout the world. The imagery of American popular culture is the lingua franca of international commerce, but with only minor variations and exceptions, Yankee color use bears a striking resemblance to that of its pan-European origins. In fact, in any country that has regular contact with the rest of the world, these conventions of color significance are understood.

Meanings in Western Countries

However complex and contradictory its meanings, black is always to be taken seriously. This is the color of death and of mourning. Widows throughout European society have traditionally worn black for a long period of mourning, if not the rest of their lives. It is the color of the unknown; something to be feared. It is also lugubrious, luxurious, ominous and impenetrable. Black absorbs and retains light and heat. Black is also closely tied with the darker aspects of witchcraft—Black Mass, black cats, etc. Black commands respect, if not fear, and can be intimidating. Simply attaching the word black to something endows it with malevolence; an evil person is said to have a black heart, a black mood is not a good one, etc. Black can mean sobriety, and the self-imposed austerity of priests, punks, and artists. Fuel in its most potent form (oil, coal) is black. Black is also a symbol of elegance, sophistication, and nobility, worn by the highborn of Europe since Spanish nobility set the fashion in the 16th century. A black tie event calls for formal wear; a black automobile sends the message that its owner is serious, powerful, and may be from the upper classes.

White generally means purity, cleanliness, and goodness. It can also stand for emptiness and blankness; it may mean neutrality, the absence of color, like an unpainted canvas. Nurses' uniforms and doctors' smocks are usually white. White packaging is common for dairy products, conveying as it does hygiene and freshness. White can also mean antiseptic—too clean; germ-free, sterile, lifeless. A white flag signals a truce or surrender.

Often pointed to as lacking color or character, gray is remarkably multifaceted, changing according to its texture and its context. It is the color of stone, of cathedrals and ancient buildings. As the color of concrete and steel, it is also the tone of modern architecture and the industrial age. It is the color of fog, a cousin to the void of black or white; a gray area is defined by its ambiguity. It is the color of aftermath; of rubble and ash, of smoke and spent fuel. The brain is referred to as gray matter. Gray implies age, experience, and wisdom. Grays are considered tasteful and sophisticated for clothing and cars.

Brushed silver implies technology and has decidedly masculine overtones, including shaving implements with their evocations of swords and other weaponry. Polished silver generally tends to mean objects that, while useful, are finely crafted and expensive. Knights of medieval times whose heraldic colors included silver were conveying not only their faith and purity, but their ability to afford silver. Zinc or brushed aluminum are often stand-ins for brushed silver.

According to the poet William Butler Yeats, red is "the color of magic in every country and has been so from the earliest times." For this reason, red is a sexy color for clothing and cars, and red roses signify romantic love. Psychologists associate red with optimism, extraversion, impulsiveness, and vigor. Since the early 20th century, it has indicated Communism. Red conveys full and strong flavor. On international signage, red indicates a prohibition of movement, the possibility of danger, and a warning to use extreme caution.

Because of its high visibility, yellow is a popular background for banners and signs, and many countries use it for mailboxes, telephone booths, and sources of reference (the telephone yellow pages, information kiosks in airports, etc.). Yellow may also indicate a potential hazard. In its role as a stand-in for gold, yellow packaging can signify a premium product, particularly in food packaging.

████████

The color of the sky. The Christian heaven is represented as being in the sky; this gives the color spiritual significance, and the implications of fidelity, serenity, and truth. Blue indicates trustworthiness, reliability, peace of mind, and contentment. Psychologically speaking, blue indicates introspection, responsibility, conservatism, culture, and spirituality.

Blue has a rare and precious significance in the natural world, whether in robins' eggs, turquoise, or lapis lazuli. Blue's implications change along with its shade; lighter blues tend toward positive and happy meanings, medium blue get more serious (trustworthy, reliable, etc.), and darker blue might mean the danger of an approaching storm or deep water. Dark blue has similar meanings to black, but is less sinister; it is mysterious and romantic—even seductive—but not deadly. As pale blue represents the sky, dark blue represents the sea; the dress uniforms of most navies are dark (navy) blue. To have "the blues" is to be depressed; Picasso's blue period (1901-1904), is often assumed to reflect his emotional state of the time.

████████

Green symbolizes nature and fertility; it evokes crops and gardens (including the Garden of Eden) and therefore survival and abundance. A successful gardener is said to have a green thumb. Until white became standard, brides wore green wedding dresses in the hope of fecundity; and the king and queen of pagan May Day festivals were bedecked in green, symbolizing spring and rebirth. Green is a restful color to the eye, and psychologists believe that it conveys clarity and certainty, elicits confidence, and implies emotional balance. Ironically, it is also the color associated with envy and jealousy. The Green Party in European politics emphasizes environmental issues, and the word "green" alone has become nearly synonymous with ecology. Contemporary surgeons wear green scrubs; many armies use green for camouflage combat wear. Green has its negative side. When someone looks "green" they are unwell. Mold, mildew, algae, slime and decay are green. Green also holds the implications of being untried, inexperienced, bumbling, unripe, young, and not worthy of serious consideration.

████████

The high visibility of orange against any background makes it useful for life rafts and vests, roadside advertising, and warning signs where it indicates dangerous equipment that may cut, crush, or shock. Orange has a taint of the cheap about it; it is frequently cited as a least-favorite color. Things that are naturally orange—ginger cats, autumn leaves, oranges, day lilies—have virtually no negative connotations, and once held a whiff of exoticism because of their rarity. Orange is considered a loud color and one of questionable taste.

████████

Brown has mostly positive meanings, with a rather masculine characteristic. Thought of as a virtual non-color because of its ubiquitousness in nature, it is earthy and strong, but also humble and practical. It describes all sorts of wood, soil, and animal fur, and by itself can be fairly meaningless until defined further as light or dark, along with whatever other color it tends toward (red, gold, etc.). Wood tones alone run from nearly white to virtually black, and often the name of a specific type of wood is used for all instances of that color (mahogany, cherry). Topaz denotes friendship and fidelity.

The expense of creating this color, combined with its rarity in nature, has given purple a particular aura for centuries. The difficulty of producing a fast, deep purple was so great that the dyes and resulting cloth were nearly as precious as gold, making this a color most used by royalty or the rich. The color still holds implications of nobility and luxury—the Royal Purple. It also evokes power and spirituality, love of truth, and nostalgia. Psychologists associate the color with a good mind, wit, and vanity. In medieval times it was supposed to have medicinal and magical qualities. The stone amethyst was once thought to be a love potion, to sharpen intelligence and to cure or prevent drunkenness; in fact amethyst in Greek means not drunk and the stone was used as a hangover cure.

Pink has predominantly positive associations, but is delicate, lacking the power and strength of red; it is the color of flirtation, not of passion. It is considered a feminine color (although not as adamantly in Europe as in the United States), the color of sensitivity and feeling. In many countries baby girls are dressed in pink. It is the color of lips, the color of a blush. A soothing color, soft tones of pink are often used for interior decor.

Gold has a mystical quality. It is so valuable that it transcends the realm of color. In most Western countries a pale gold is preferred (darker gold is preferred in Italy and Asia). Gold implies luxury and money to burn. The use of gold for decor is viewed as extravagant, even a bit excessive. Still it is used, and often quite openly, as a display of wealth.

England, Scotland, Wales and Ireland

The United Kingdom
The flag of the United Kingdom is the Union Jack, which combines the flags of England, Scotland, Wales, and Northern Ireland. It is one of the world's most recognized symbols.

Scotland
The Scottish flag features the cross of St. Andrews on a field of blue, which is the national color. This flag forms the background of the Union Jack.

Ireland
One of the many flags inspired by the French tricolor, the color symbolism of Ireland's national banner has green standing for the catholic majority, orange honoring the Protestant King William III, and white representing peace.

Before the sun set on the British Empire, boatloads of booty had been brought back to the mother country. Much of this treasure wasn't gold or precious gems, but fabrics and the dyes with which to color them. The volume and longevity of Great Britain's international commerce and colonialism also gave the country a taste for, and familiarity with, the ways of the world beyond its shores. Imports both transformed and were transformed by the country—what could be more British than tea, curry, and khaki?

For the most part, British color conventions fit the European model and draw from many of the same sources. The United Kingdom's slight remove—psychologically as well as physically—from the rest of the continent has added color traditions unique to Britons, starting with the ancient Druidic color hierarchy: Green represented wisdom, blue truth, and white purity.

The color representative of the monarchy, and by extension, the state, red is the color of power and authority. Mailboxes are red, a tradition that persists even in many former British colonies, signifying that mail delivery is a government task. The carpets in the law courts are red, as are the judge's robes, again signifying the authority of the crown. The dress uniform of several branches of the British military is red. The red rose was emblematic of the house of Tudor. Until the late 19th century, English physicians wore red cloaks, and red flannel was thought to have medicinal properties when applied as a poultice. Red wool was used to relieve sprains in Scotland and sore throats in Ireland. The red and white diagonally striped barber pole is a holdover from the days when the local barber also practiced some surgical procedures, his skill with a blade being handy. Red is also the color of London buses and telephone booths, which benefit from the positive association of reliability and visibility that the color conveys. Red is also the color of jackets worn in traditional English fox hunts. In Ireland and elsewhere in the world red hair is commonly associated with the Irish fiery temper.

Yellow, the color of rain slickers, is associated with items made of rubber, as it was once the only color in which rubber was available.

The Order of the Garter, a ribbon bestowed for valiant services to the country, is blue. Wedgwood blue, a tranquil, dignified, powdery medium blue, is emblematic of the Georgian era, and with British refinement and decorum. The double-breasted dark blue blazer began as part of the British naval uniform. London Blue Topaz is the dark shade of the popular gemstone.

Scottish warriors painted themselves blue, partly because they had the paint and partly because they hoped that it would frighten or confuse their enemies. It is no coincidence that blue is the traditional color for Scottish sporting teams.

In a nation of enthusiastic gardeners green has mostly positive associations, including Green Man pubs; Robin Hood; forests and farmland; and the berets worn by the elite Royal Marines. Bottles of green glass imply a high quality product within. British Racing Green, emblematic of high-performance cars manufactured in Britain, is a deep blue-green. The color is identified with the Irish St. Patrick. Ireland's national color is green, and kelly green is emblematic of the country's catholic majority and is recognized worldwide. The leprechaun and the four-leaf clover, both universally associated with Ireland, are popular green icons.

Soil has positive connotations, and so does brown. It signifies honesty, lack of pretension, and manual labor.

The colors of royalty, gold and purple, are the colors of the royal crown.

The color of mourning and undertakers and death, as is true throughout the Western world. Black in Britain is also a common color for clothing, and a standard for anyone wishing to appear dignified, although all-black outfits became synonymous with the punk movement of the 1970s. As with Catholic priests, Anglican clerics wear black. In London, taxis are black. Jet, a hard black stone made from lignite, a variety of coal, that takes a high shine was popularly used in jewelry, particularly during the Victorian era; it was manufactured in Yorkshire, England, a town popular for its local lignite.

The points of the compass were color-coded by the ancient Irish: north is black; south is white; east is purple; and west is brownish-gray.
The upper classes have long favored white clothing for leisure and sportswear, perhaps as a display that they can afford to have it cleaned. The color for English sporting teams is traditionally white. The famous chalk cliffs of Dover are white. White is also associated with Ireland's renowned white linen and lace. In Ireland, white also stands for peace.

The early 19th century dandy Beau Brummel favored dove gray; he established the idea that subdued clothing is sophisticated and elegant. The idea has largely stuck, and gray is considered classy, traditional, and tasteful, if perhaps a bit safe. A light shade of gray is associated with Cambridge, while Oxford gray is a darker charcoal. In architecture, paler grays can indicate stately old stone buildings and, therefore, the solidity of long-standing institutions; darker grays may intone the grim, gritty look of an industrial town.

Represented in Ireland s flag, orange symbolizes the Protestant religion.

WHITE HOT

Open a newspaper of the 1920s or early 1930s and the bulk of jewelry advertisements for wedding sets promoted platinum bands. However, during World War II, many countries, including the U.S., prohibited the use of platinum in non-military applications. Because platinum was preferred but unavailable, jewelry manufacturers mixed alloys with yellow gold to create white gold, which mimicked the look of platinum. Yellow gold was also used more in its natural state and subsequently, became the choice for traditional wedding sets during the latter half of the century. As the 20th century drew to a close, white metals—silver, white gold, and platinum, were rediscovered and once again, became popular choices for wedding sets and all kinds of jewelry.

66 · 67

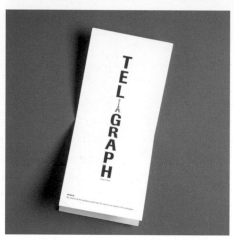

The Telegraph Colour Library wanted to present its identity guidelines interestingly enough to actually get read. To meet this objective, HGV Design Consultants created a booklet that is simple, fun, and to the point. It also makes use of color—most notably, yellow. Designers chose yellow for its modern and fresh appeal, and because it reflected the diversity of the images in the library's range and linked the images with words.

The inside pages are stripped of color, focusing on the Telegraph logo and spotlighting a different four-color image from its library. Many of the images are subtle in color, including steely shades of gray as shown in photos of a multi-tool, an elephant, and the Eiffel Tower. When boldly colored images are used, such as the traditional English red phone booth—the images literally pop off the page.

PROJECT   TELEGRAPH COLOUR LIBRARY IDENTITY
                 GUIDELINES
DESIGN FIRM   HGV DESIGN CONSULTANTS
ART DIRECTORS   PIERRE VERMEIR, JIM SUTHERLAND
DESIGNER   DOMINIC EDMUNDS
PHOTOGRAPHER   JOHN EDWARDS
PRINTER   MAXIM
CLIENT   TELEGRAPH COLOUR LIBRARY

HERALDIC COLORS

The precursor to flags, military uniforms, regimental banners, and corporate logos, medieval heraldry introduced the first widespread secular use of symbolic color and standardized color meaning outside the church, although most heraldic color symbolism was harmonized with that of the church. Heraldry was developed as a way to distinguish between armor-plated combatants on the battlefield. Color was only a part of the heraldic scheme, designating a knight's place in the aristocratic hierarchy or his allegiances. Early on the rule of two colors per blazon was established. Red stood for courage, zeal, and sacrifice; blue meant piety and sincerity; orange or tan signified strength and endurance; yellow meant honor and loyalty; green represented faith and youth. Silver stood for purity and faith, and in England was reserved for use only by higher nobility; purple signified royalty and high rank; brown was used by lesser nobles; black stood for penitence and grief; and gold was reserved for royalty only. During the Crusades, French soldiers wore red crosses on their shoulders; the Flemish wore green crosses; English soldiers wore white crosses.

Unlike most letterheads that use color sparingly, usually for just the type and logo, or take the reverse approach and use a colored sheet of paper, HGV Design Consultants opted for a letterhead design that floods nearly half the paper with bold color. Designers reversed the type and a cloud out of a true blue hue. The designer chose blue to "lay the cloud upon" because it matches the color of the sky, which is seen as being light and clean—two attributes they wanted to associate with Neo, a manufacturer of modern furniture in the UK, whick markets to Europe.

PROJECT	NEO LETTERHEAD
DESIGN FIRM	HGV DESIGN CONSULTANTS
ART DIRECTORS/	
DESIGNERS	JIM SUTHERLAND, PIERRE VERMEIR
PRINTER	CTD
CLIENT	NEO

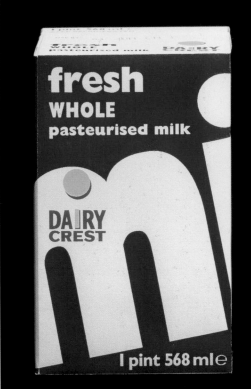

■ ■ ■ Charged with reinforcing a well-known British dairy company's image as an innovative marketer, Carter Wong created a package design system that stands out from the competition. Because it adheres to the color coding of dairy products in Britain—whole milk in a blue carton, semi-skimmed in green, and skimmed in red—the bold, clean graphics are recognizable to the public.

PROJECT   DAIRY CREST PACKAGING
DESIGN FIRM   CARTER WONG & PARTNERS
CLIENT   DAIRY CREST

Western Europe

For the redesign of its mens' grooming line for the European market, Gillette wanted to evoke masculinity, cleanliness, and innovation. Desgrippes Gobé transposed the masculine, high-tech brushed-steel surface of the company's best-selling razor onto the plastic containers of its aftershave colognes and deodorants. Blue and green were used for the labels because of their associations with freshness and cleanliness.

PROJECT	GILLETTE MENS' SHAVING PRODUCT PACKAGING
DESIGN FIRM	DESGRIPPES GOBÉ & ASSOCIATES
CLIENT	GILLETTE

Global Graphics: Colors

■ The Ian Logan Design Co.'s choice of shiny, black bags
help bring the bright labels to the forefront. The black
packaging also adds a touch of sophistication and class.

PROJECT   GOURMET COFFEE PACKAGING
DESIGN FIRM   IAN LOGAN DESIGN CO.

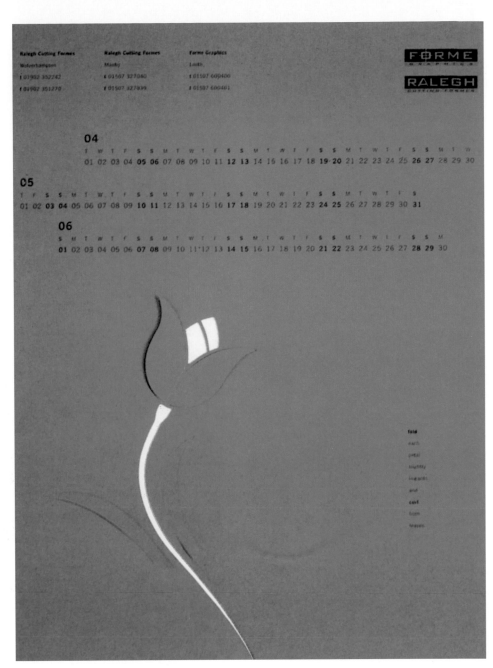

By reversing a normal color scheme, the long yellow silhouette of the flower stem is emphasized against a green background. The quantity of green also offers a friendly, expansive sense of warmth—as if from a grassy field.

PROJECT   FORME GRAPHICS, RALEGH CUTTING FORMES
                   CALENDAR SELF-PROMOTION
DESIGN FIRM   WPA PINFOLD
ART DIRECTORS   MYLES PINFOLD, RICHARD HEARST
CLIENT   FORME GRAPHICS, RALEGH CUTTING FORMES

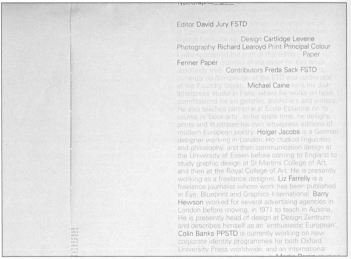

Editor David Jury FSTD

Design Cartlidge Levene
Photography Richard Learoyd Print Principal Colour
Paper
Fenner Paper Contributors Freda Sack FSTD is
currently co-chairperson at the STD and co-director
of the Foundry Studio. Michael Caine runs his own
letterpress studio in Paris, where he works on book
commissions for art galleries, publishers and writers.
He also teaches part-time at Ecole Estienne on its
course in 'book-arts'. In his spare time, he designs,
prints and illustrates his own letterpress editions of
modern European poetry. Holger Jacobs is a German
designer working in London. He studied linguistics
and philosophy, and then communication design at
the University of Essen before coming to England to
study graphic design at St Martins College of Art,
and then at the Royal College of Art. He is presently
working as a freelance designer. Liz Farrelly is a
freelance journalist whose work has been published
in Eye, Blueprint and Graphics International. Barry
Hewson worked for several advertising agencies in
London before moving, in 1971 to teach in Austria.
He is presently head of design at Design Zentrum
and describes himself as an 'enthusiastic European'.
Colin Banks PPSTD is currently working on new
corporate identity programmes for both Oxford
University Press worldwide, and an international

TypoGraphic 51 explores the dissolving of international boundaries, gathering contributions from designers, educators, and writers practicing worldwide. Designed to be viewed as both a bound thirty-two page A4 journal and a double-sided 2XA1 poster, its blue typography and coloration lend a spirit of calm and continuity to experiments with communication and transgression across traditional constraints.

PROJECT **TYPOGRAPHIC 51 JOURNAL**
DESIGN FIRM **CARTLIDGE LEVENE**
CREATIVE DIRECTOR **IAN CARTLIDGE**
DESIGNER **PHILIP COSTIN, IAN STYLES, HUGH TARPEY, EMMA WEBB**
PHOTOGRAPHER **RICHARD LEAROYD**
CLIENT **INTERNATIONAL SOCIETY OF TYPOGRAPHIC DESIGNERS**

Accept no minimal existence

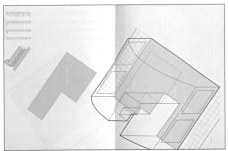

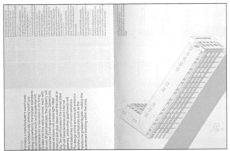

ANGEL STATION

To design a promotional brochure and identity for marketing the Canal Building, Cartlidge Levene focused on the diversity of the local area, the rich array of amenities accessible to potential residents, and the building's waterside location. Throughout the brochure, a many-hued wash of blue, including blue type, reinforces the allure of waterfront living. A subtle duotone applied the original building pictured on the gatefold, suggests its transformation.

PROJECT	CANAL BUILDING BROCHURE
DESIGN FIRM	CARTLIDGE LEVENE
CREATIVE DIRECTOR	IAN CARTLIDGE
DESIGNERS	PHILIP COSTIN, IAN STYLES, HUGH TARPEY, EMMA WEBB
PHOTOGRAPHER	RICHARD LEAROYD
TECHNICAL DRAWINGS	JOHN HEWITT
CLIENT	MILLENNIUM LOFTS

Report **Alex Kershaw** Photographs **Charles Ommanney**

God's inmates

Imagine a rehabilitation system so successful that a prisoner refuses
to released before he has completed its Christian programme. Only in
America, you might think. But it is already here – in three British jails

■ Wayne Ford, art director and designer for London's *The
Observer Magazine*, chose brown to complement the
black-and-white photography in this editorial spread.
"Brown reflects the earth, naturalness, goodness, and a
fresh new start for the prison inmates in this story,"
Ford said. "Brown gives the story an uplifting feel without overpowering the images.

PROJECT	THE OBSERVER MAGAZINE
	"GOD'S INMATES" ARTICLE
DESIGN FIRM	THE OBSERVER MAGAZINE
ART DIRECTOR/	
DESIGNER	WAYNE FORD
PHOTOGRAPHER	CHARLES OMMANNEY
COPYWRITER	SHERYL GARRATT
PRINTER	QUEBECOR
CLIENT	THE OBSERVER MAGAZINE

■ Bessi Karavil designed this identity system for ESL Ceramics, a company based in London that produces ceramics. She opted for brown as the primary hue for the one-color identity because it represents the natural color of the clay before it is painted and fired. "I enriched the logo's visibility using a 'tile shape' relief in the stationery set. I also spread small tiles on the paper using a matt paint," explained Karavil.

PROJECT	**ESL CERAMICS IDENTITY SYSTEM**
DESIGN FIRM	**STUDIO KARAVIL**
ART DIRECTOR/	
DESIGNER	**BESSI KARAVIL**
PRINTER	**NUOVO POLISTYGEGRAF**
CLIENT	**ESL CERAMICS**

■ A vibrant orange was the color of choice for Arc Dance Company's business card, a London-based firm that markets itself throughout the UK and Europe. Designers chose orange for the vibrancy, warmth, and passion inherent in the shade—qualities easily equated with contemporary dance. Likewise, they staged the photography of the dancers, contained in the letter C of the company's name, to reflect the drama and diversity of the troupe.

PROJECT   ARC DANCE COMPANY BUSINESS CARD
DESIGN FIRM   HGV DESIGN CONSULTANTS
ART DIRECTORS/
DESIGNERS   JIM SUTHERLAND, PIERRE VERMEIR
PHOTOGRAPHER   SHEILA ROCK
PRINTER   CTD
CLIENT   ARC DANCE COMPANY

France

In French culture, a vibrant, broad spectrum of hues is freely utilized.

The French tricolor flag is the symbol of the Republic, an icon of great significance that stirs the heart of every patriotic French citizen. Like its cousins in the U.S. and Great Britain, it is used to sell anything and everything.

The high profile of the arts and fashion in French society makes them useful points of reference for anyone designing for the country today. Particular colors and combinations of colors can be representative of specific time periods and can be used to evoke a given era or an individual artist or artistic movement. The country is one of color. Its northern coast, famous for the Normandy shoreline, is agricultural—a mix of blue water, rocky landscapes, and greenery. Paris is the City of Light—boasting dozens of museums full of color from collective works of Degas, Cezanne, Gauguin, Van Gogh, Seurat, and Renoir in the Louvre to the golden décor of the Palace of Versailles to the colorful hues Henri de Toulouse-Lautrec's paintings, inspired by Paris's Montmartre district, the center of the cabaret entertainment, and bohemian life. South of Paris, one ventures into the wine and Champagne regions with a palette of lush vegetation. The southern coast has an array of warm colors, accented by the colorful color-coded umbrellas that dot the Mediterranean shoreline.

The color of blood, red signifies passion, love, and lust, lips and skin flushed with excitement. Renowned French fashion designer Coco Chanel immortalized bright red lipstick. Flags of rebellion have been red, notably during the French Revolution. Aristocrats who survived the rein of terror after the Revolution wore red scarves around their necks. France's blue, white, and red flag is the symbol of the republic, an icon of great significance that stirs the heart of every patriotic French citizen. Like its counterparts in the U.S. and Great Britain, the French flag is used to sell anything and everything.

Often a substitute for gold in terms of symbolic meaning, yellow has positive associations with flowers, summer, and joy; it has also been badly tainted by its association with betrayal. The color is inescapably linked to delicious foods: lemons and other citrus fruits, bananas, egg yolks, butter, and cheese. Mailboxes in France are yellow. A yellow or gold fleur-de-lis on a blue or purple background has been the French royal insignia since the Middle Ages.

La Cote d'Azur, the southern coastline of France between Marceilles and Nice, gets its name for its deep blue sea. The water is remarkably blue against the white sands. It is calming, soothing, and upscale. Parisian street signs are blue with white lettering. Guerlain's perfume "L'Heure Bleu" is named for twilight, an hour of the day considered very romantic. What is now known as the Hope Diamond, an 112 3/16 carat blue diamond, was purchased by a French merchant who sold the stone to King Louis XIV of France in 1668. The diamond was re-cut and became part of the French Crown Jewels. Because of its steely blue/violet color, it was known as the Blue Diamond of the Crown as well as the French Blue.

"French Green" is a deep blue-green, common on Parisian park chairs. Shutters of a somewhat warmer green are characteristic. The pale, powdery gray-green of oxidized copper or bronze is typical of the rooftops of Parisian buildings. Absinthe green is a cloudy, yellowish green named after a potent 19th century liquor.

The French monarchy was among the first secular European powers to use gold for large-scale decorative purposes. France's great palaces, such as the Palace of Versailles, are ornately decorated in gold. Pale shades of gold also signify French champagne, which comes from the Champagne region of the country. Paris is known as the City of Light.

Orange, a region in the south of France, is known for its orange-y/brown earth. Pottery and figures made of this rich shade of golden brown can be found everywhere and are popular with tourists who buy them as souvenirs. The word orange comes from the Old French *orange*.

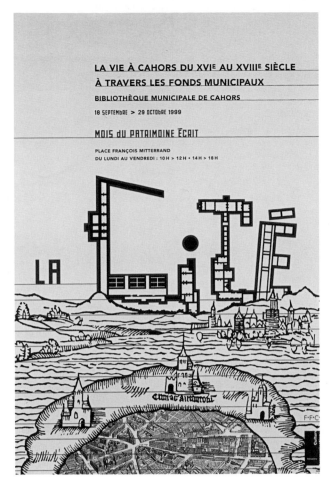

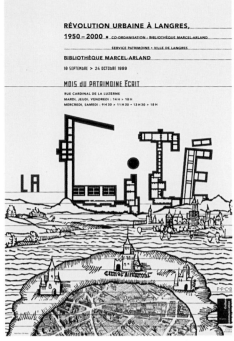

Each of these four posters, promoting a series of month-long exhibitions in different towns throughout France, uses different pastel colors to symbolize historical documents—patrimoine écrit—loosely translated means inheritance of the written word. Designers Muriel Paris and Alex Singer chose the pastel hues of light yellow, blue, and pink as a tribute to France's past.

PROJECT	MOIS DU PATRIMOINE ÉCRIT
DESIGN FIRM	MURIEL PARIS AND ALEX SINGER
ART DIRECTORS/	
DESIGNERS/	
ILLUSTRATORS	MURIEL PARIS AND ALEX SINGER
CLIENT	FFCB (FÉDERATION FRANÇAISE DE COOPERATION ENTRE LES BIBLIOTHÈQUES)

Nearly complementary, blue and gold have been a favorite color combination since ancient Egypt. The high visibility of gold's yellow hue is enhanced when placed against a background of blue. In addition, each color carries various meanings and nuances; blue can conjure up anything from royalty to romance; gold is almost universally a color associated with objects of desire.

For these reasons, Desgrippe Gobé chose this palette for these upmarket fragrances—one for women, one for men—for the Parisian jeweler Boucheron. The women's scent uses a bracelet shape with a gold accent, topped off in a sapphire color, the company's signature stone. The bottle for the men's cologne uses the same colors in similar proportions but in an architectural form, giving it a more masculine character. For either gender, the gold suggests value, preciousness, and luxury, and the blue evokes mystery, elegance, and romance. The deep, lush blue of the print ad lends a sensual touch.

PROJECT   BOUCHERON PERFUME PACKAGING
DESIGN FIRM   DESGRIPPE GOBÉ

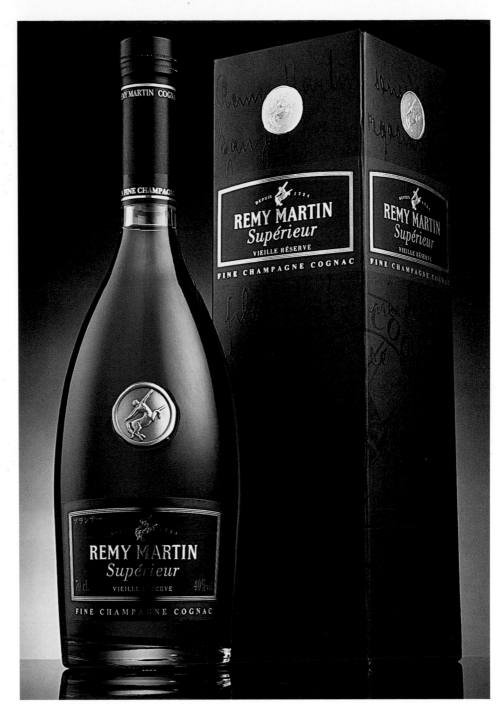

Rémy Martin's new packaging by Carré Noir serves as a
jewel box. Black and gold are the company's traditional colors and are synonymous with luxury. The box's
rich copper-brown background implies age, authentici-
ty and pedigree, and heightens the effect of the bottle's
rich color.

PROJECT   RÉMY MARTIN COGNAC PACKAGING
DESIGN FIRM   CARRÉ NOIR

Global Graphics: Colors

■ ■ ■ ■ Carré Noir developed a program of packaging for Jacques Vabre coffee following the conventional logic of color coding foods. Red conveys strength of flavor; blue indicates decaffeinated coffee. The red-orange and black of the Gringo blend not only evokes Latin America, but robust, rich flavor with a hint of the exotic. A mild cream-flavored blend is packed in a range of beiges to convey its smoother taste, while mimicking the actual color of coffee with cream.

PROJECT   JACQUES VABRE COFFEE PACKAGING
DESIGN FIRM   CARRÉ NOIR

■ The green label of Danone aloe vera yogurt expresses
several ideas connected with green that are in keeping
with the marketing strategy for this food product
nature, freshness, health, and rejuvenation.

PROJECT   **DANONE ALOE VERA YOGURT PACKAGING**
DESIGN FIRM   **CARRÉ NOIR**

■ Although red is considered vital, virile, and masculine throughout Europe, it is rarely used for shaving products because of the obvious connection to blood. Carré Noir convinced Vichy Laboratories to run counter to this convention and make red the signature color of its mens' shaving line. The resulting packaging stands out vividly against the blue and green tones of the competition.

PROJECT   VICHY LABRORATORIES SHAVING PACKAGING
DESIGN FIRM   CARRÉ NOIR

A range of 3M protective gear for workers (ear plugs, air filters, etc.) uses a gradation of blue on its packaging as a unifying element. Because the products were to be sold throughout thirty Western and Eastern European countries, blue was chosen because of its overwhelming popularity and widespread connotations of reliability and trust.

PROJECT   3M PROTECTIVE GEAR PACKAGING
DESIGN FIRM CARRÉ NOIR

Global Graphics: Colors

Une nouvelle idée du maquillage
A new vision of makeup

Dior

When asked to create a press to as part of Christian Dior's launch of a new cosmetic product called, "Lumière Noire," Fabrice Praeger designed a kit using a purple light bulb—in other words, a black light, *lumière noire* in French. Black lights had their heyday in the 1960s, and consequently, are associated with the culture of that decade. Today, they are popular in discotheques in Europe and elsewhere. Black lights and their purple hue are associated with dancing, parties, and sex, because of the exotic, somewhat dubious atmosphere that results when they are turned on. A black light begs the question, "Is what you see real or isn't it?"

Such is the case with this Christian Dior makeup—invisible when worn in traditional lighting; white when activated under lumière noire. To graphically illustrate the product's features, Praeger used a black light as the primary graphic—a purple lightbulb. But the key to the kit's success, is a black-and-white photograph of a woman's face wearing Lumière Noire in traditional light. Pull out the page, and the image changes to show what the same face looks like under black light. "Using a bank-notes detector, I added the copy 'Detector of girls who are wearing Lumière Noire make-up.' I created [it as] a gag, but maybe it is not as silly as it seems," said Praeger.

The mystery and allure of the black light brings to mind the old advertising slogan for a popular American haircolor, "Does she or doesn't she?" In this case, only under a black light will you know for sure.

PROJECT   CHRISTIAN DIOR LUMIÈRE NOIRE PRESS KIT
DESIGN FIRM   FABRICE PRAEGER
ART DIRECTOR/
DESIGNER/
COPYWRITER   FABRICE PRAEGER
PHOTOGRAPHER   TYEN (CHRISTIAN DIOR)
CLIENT   CHRISTIAN DIOR

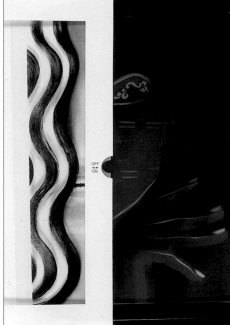

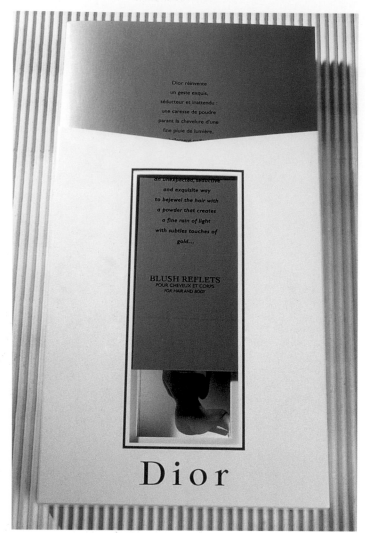

Dior

Dior

Dior

■ Gold and golden tones form the color palette for Christian Dior's new Blush Reflets, a powder makeup applied to the body and particularly, to the hair. Christian Dior, an upscale cosmetic manufacturer, has built its reputation on quality products and high-end presentation, so gold, the color of the product's brush and a symbol of luxury, is key to the press kit's color scheme. Fabrice Praeger's concept for the kit arose from the idea that the hairs on the brush could be used to make a flat photographic image appear three-dimensional. When the press kit or box is opened, a golden figure of a nude woman is slowly revealed. When the pull-out is completely extended, the entire figure is shown, along with the woman's luxurious hair, which is actually the makeup brush. The presentation is opulent and luxury is implied. This is a product a woman would gravitate to when she wanted to pamper herself.

PROJECT CHRISTIAN DIOR BLUSH REFLETS PRESS KIT
DESIGN FIRM FABRICE PRAEGER
ART DIRECTOR/
DESIGNER/
COPYWRITER FABRICE PRAEGER
PHOTOGRAPHER PHOTOTÈQUE
CLIENT CHRISTIAN DIOR

Paris is a city known for its greenery, but that wasn't enough for Le Pari Vert (green Paris), an organization whose goal it is to make Paris even more green by planting trees on streets and balconies. When asked to create a logo for the effort, Fabrice Praeger designed a green leaf, complete with veins. The veins outline a map of Paris, including the Seine River that divides the city. Beneath the logo, the line of text means, "Let's recover our roots."

PROJECT	LE PARI VERT LOGO
DESIGN FIRM	FABRICE PRAEGER
ART DIRECTOR/	
DESIGNER/	
ILLUSTRAPHER/	
COPYWRITER	FABRICE PRAEGER
CIENT	LE PARI VERT ASSOCIATION

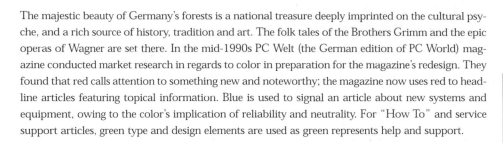

Germany, Austria, and Switzerland

Germany, Austria, and Switzerland are influenced by the deep greens and vivid blues of the forests and alpine regions.

Germany
The flag of Germany is composed of three horizontal stripes; from top to bottom, black, red and yellow. While not sacrosanct, the flag and this combination of colors are not widely used for commercial purposes.

Austria
The Austrian flag features a coat of arms on a field of red and white.

Switzerland
The Swiss flag has become synonymous with neutrality and was the model for the banner of the International Red Cross, in part because of that organization's wish to be seen as non-combatant during wartime.

The majestic beauty of Germany's forests is a national treasure deeply imprinted on the cultural psyche, and a rich source of history, tradition and art. The folk tales of the Brothers Grimm and the epic operas of Wagner are set there. In the mid-1990s PC Welt (the German edition of PC World) magazine conducted market research in regards to color in preparation for the magazine's redesign. They found that red calls attention to something new and noteworthy; the magazine now uses red to headline articles featuring topical information. Blue is used to signal an article about new systems and equipment, owing to the color's implication of reliability and neutrality. For "How To" and service support articles, green type and design elements are used as green represents help and support.

Alpine snowcapped mountains have come to be associated with the tourist trade. Alpine resorts, popular with skiing enthusiasts, are especially prevalent in Austria and Switzerland and contribute greatly to the economy. White is also the color of edelweiss, a rare small white velvety flower found in the alps and made famous in the film The Sound of Music.

Blue is a shade that symbolizes reliability and neutrality. It also has its romantic overtones and has immortalized the Danube River in the popular waltz The Blue Danube. Swiss Blue Topaz is a common name that refers to a medium shade of the blue topaz gemstone with a Sky Blue Topaz being lighter hue and London Blue being the darkest.

For most of the 20th century, the color of German phone booths and mailboxes was yellow. When the national phone company privatized, all phone booths were changed to a vivid magenta overnight. Although announced beforehand, it was still a shock to much of the population; however, the revamped utility proved reliable and innovative. In times of active persecution, European Jews were forced to wear yellow, most notoriously yellow Stars of David in the 1930s and 1940s.

To many, the emblematic color of Germany is metallic gray, equally recognizable in a Mercedes-Benz or a Braun electric shaver.

The deep greens and vivid blues of the alpine regions are virtually national colors. They also figure in the local color lexicon. While the finest emeralds come from Columbia, they are also mined in Austria.

Equated with money and wealth throughout the world, it can also be equated with Swiss bank accounts.

Aside from its implications with the earth and soil, brown is universally recognized as the color of rich Swiss chocolate.

With a wink at Surrealism and the optical phenomenon of after-image, an Austrian fashion retailer named Blue gets orange—its opposite on the color wheel—as the key color in the store's signs, interiors, shopping bags, and ads. "With a name like Blue, we just had to do it in orange," said Stefan Sagmeister.

Once established as the company's signature color, the subsequent ad campaign relied on a consistent spot of orange within a richly textured black-and-white photo of an oblique visual pun on blue things (eyes, earth as seen from space, etc.) such as the blues, seen here. Because the budget was limited and it afforded no room for hiring beautiful fashion models, "We just took our ugly friends and put bags over their heads," said Sagmeister. The campaign was incredibly successful. Three weeks after the opening of the first three stores, the client stated that his only problem with the campaign was that the stores' merchandise was sold out.

PROJECT	BLUE IDENTITY CAMPAIGN
DESIGN FIRM	SAGMEISTER INC.
ART DIRECTOR/ DESIGNER	STEFAN SAGMEISTER
DIGITAL ART	KAMIL VOJNAR
PHOTOGRAPHER	TOM SCHIERLITZ
COPYWRITER	STEFAN SAGMEISTER
BACKGROUNDS	JUDITH EISLER
PRINTER	VORARLKERGER VERLAGSANSTALT
CLIENT	BLUE/MARTIN SAGMEISTER

■ ■ Udings-Hof's "Living in the Garden" brochure takes
consumers there—to the garden—with a palette of
deep green leafy shades accented with natural hues of
brown and terra cotta, all of which stands out on a
background of white. Dirk Rullkötter's color choices
were deliberately chosen to recreate the colors and
atmosphere found in a garden.

PROJECT   LIVING IN THE GARDEN BROCHURE
DESIGN FIRM   RULLKÖTTER AGD
ART DIRECTOR   DIRK RULLKÖTTER
CLIENT   UDINGS-HOF

German designer Dirk Rullkötter relied on a bold, apple shade of red to create a corporate identity system that makes an innovative and strong impression for his client, !EVO Online Marketing GmbH, which wanted to send a loud signal to its target market in Germany and internationally. In this design, red conveys daring, creative thinking, and assertiveness, all of which is enhanced with use of bold type and thick black lines. Traditionally, white space appears as a passive design element, but here, the white becomes an active design participant, holding its own with the red.

PROJECT	**!EVO ONLINE MARKETING GMBH CORPORATE IDENTITY**
DESIGN FIRM	**RULLKÖTTER AGD**
ART DIRECTOR	**DIRK RULLKÖTTER**
CLIENT	**!EVO ONLINE MARKETING GMBH**

Offen, zeitgemäss, transparent.
Raumatmosphäre für 400 MitarbeiterInnen.
Zu mieten im Hochhaus Phoenix.
Hardturmstrasse 3 Escher Wyss Platz Zürich.

Baumanagement und Verwaltung:
Interpool Verwaltungs AG Zollikon

Auskünfte: Telefon +41 1 389 86 26
www.zh-phoenix.ch

PHOENIX

This simple folder is bathed in bright yellow and features a line drawing of the Phoenix building that wraps around the spine. The rendering shows the company's headquarters in Zurich, Switzerland, which is notable for its glass tower. Hence, yellow was chosen as the color best associated with the firm because of its association with sunshine.

PROJECT	PHOENIX FOLDER
DESIGN FIRM	GOTTSCHALK + ASH INTERNATIONAL
DESIGNERS	FRITZ GOTTSCHALK, ERICH GROSS
CLIENT	I.E ENGINEERING

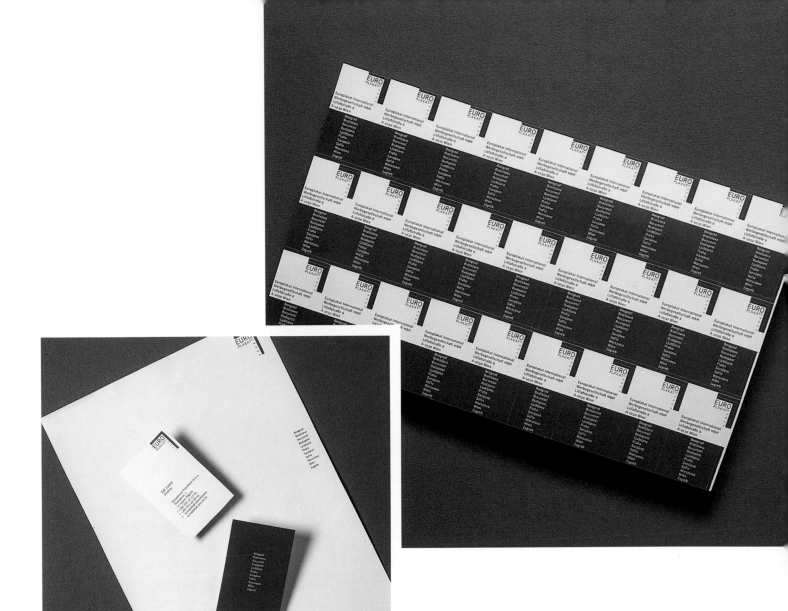

■ Why did Gottschalk + Ash International choose red as the primary color for Europlakat International, a firm that markets itself throughout Europe? Answer: Red is the color found most often in European flags. Consequently, when designers used it here on their client's letterhead, business cards, and a sheet of envelope labels, it works as a unifying element that crosses territorial borders. Europlakat International, while headquartered in Vienna, Austria, plays an equally important role in numerous other European cities including Belgrade, Bucharest, Prague, and Sarajevo.

PROJECT	EUROPLAKAT INTERNATIONAL IDENTITY SYSTEM
DESIGN FIRM	GOTTSCHALK + ASH INTERNATIONAL
DESIGNERS	FRITZ GOTTSCHALK, REGINA RODRIGUES
CLIENT	EUROPLAKAT INTERNATIONAL

Designers used royal blue accented with a golden *F* for
Freischütz for the menu and supporting materials for
this upscale Swiss restaurant because the colors are
classy according to designers—the perfect choice for
this sedate restaurant.

PROJECT	**RESTAURANT FREISCHÜTZ MENU AND IDENTITY MATERIALS**
DESIGN FIRM	**GOTTSCHALK + ASH INTERNATIONAL**
DESIGNERS	**FRITZ GOTTSCHALK, REGINA RODRIGUES**
CLIENT	**RESTAURANT FREISCHÜTZ**

Scandinavia

Iceland, Norway, Sweden, Finland

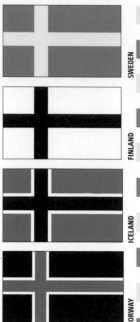

While the Scandinavian countries adhere primarily to the prevailing color conventions of Europe, combined with the regional preferences of nearby countries, it is a region of cool shade. The general rule goes: colder climate, cooler colors. Blue and white—the colors of the sky and snow—have particular resonance in Scandinavia.

The color blue has some dubious distinctions in Scandinavia. Ancient Laplanders wouldn't wear blue near a place of worship because an evil demon known to torture the dead was blue. In the Swedish variation of the Little Red Riding Hood fable, the girl's hood is not red but blue; instead of being rescued by a woodsman she is eaten by the wolf. Blue designates clean hospital supplies. In Finland, blue is slang for broke or short of money.

Green indicates germ-free sterility

In general yellow and orange are associated with heat and warmth. Mailboxes in Sweden are yellow.

Folklore in Norway has it that a white object hung outside your house will repel the devil. This region has long been a proponent of peace (it remained neutral during World War I, while Denmark and Norwy were occupied during World War II), so white is particularly significant. White is also associated with the region's icy, glacial landscape.

Viking seaman Leif Ericson, the first European to land on the North American continent and a historic figure throughout Scandinavia, was the son of Eric the Red, who was born in Iceland.

The blue and white of Finland's flag are meant to symbolize the country's lakes and snow. The other flags in the region are patterned on the same cross motif, but employ a palette of red, blue, white, and yellow.

Hyvän mielen lämmönlähde. Öljy.

FINNISH OIL and GAS
F E D E R A T I O N

(top) Öljyalan Palvelukeskus Oy (Oil Industry Service Center), an organization for oil producing companies in Finland, needed a campaign symbol that would project a positive image for oil and promote heating with oil and gas. Designers at Incognito Design Oy created the logo using red and yellow to represent warmth and clean heat. The idea came to designers from looking straight at the flames of an oil burner. In turn, they fashioned the logo to mimic the movement of the flames to represent the circulation of heat. They softened the edges by rounding and blurring the lines to project a warm, positive mood. Designers were careful to avoid blue and black; use of these colors would have made the heat appear dirty.

(bottom) Targeted throughout the Nordic countries, this logo uses an orangy-red to symbolize warmth and heat. The round shape represents both the earth and the sun as producers of clean, natural energy, while the small dots emanating from its center depict energy streaming from the sun or the earth as well as the flow of information coming from the center of an organization. To create the color seen here, designers chose a hue of red mixed with gray—red symbolizing heat while gray signifies something that exists, but is often not seen. Designers eliminated from consideration any color that didn't clearly communicate energy and warmth. Likewise, designers disregarded blue, brown, and green because they felt the colors would be too conservative and static.

PROJECT	ÖLJYALAN PALVELUKESKUS OY CAMPAIGN SYMBOL
DESIGN FIRM	INCOGNITO DESIGN OY
ART DIRECTOR/ DESIGNER	KEIJO VUORINEN
ILLUSTRATOR	ARI RANTALA
COPYWRITER	PÄIVI LARIKKO
CLIENT	ÖLJYALAN PALVELUKESKUS OY (OIL INDUSTRY SERVICE CENTER)

PROJECT	FINNISH OIL AND GAS FEDERATION LOGO
DESIGN FIRM	INCOGNITO DESIGN OY
ART DIRECTOR/ DESIGNER	KEIJO VUORINEN
ILLUSTRATOR	ARI RANTALA
CLIENT	ÖLJY — JA KAASUALAN KESKUSLIITTO RY/GM JAAKKO TUSA

Netherlands

The color of tulips—red in particular—are typically linked to the Dutch culture.

Predating the French tricolor, the flag of the Netherlands originally had an orange band across the top representing loyalty to William of Orange.

Aside from the red, white, and yellow tulips for which the region is known, the colors associated with Holland are the somber earth tones seen in its architecture, echoed in the palette of the painter Rembrandt. To characterize the culture as subdued with only occasional outbursts of accent colors might seem to make sense; but then how to explain the primary colors beloved of Piet Mondrian and the de Stijl movement?

As in Britain, red is the color of the Dutch crown, and that of many government agencies and state-run entities; mailboxes, for instance, are red. Tulips are shades of red, pink, white, and yellow.

Green is widely associated with ecology. Greenpeace, the global organization dedicated to saving the environment, is headquartered in the Netherlands, so green is synonymous with ecology.

Brown is largely seen in the Netherland's brick architecture. It is also seen in the windmills that dot the landscape, as well as in the wooden shoes that are associated with the Dutch.

Yellow is the color of cheese and butter, two of The Netherlands' primary exports. Edam and Gouda cheese are known internationally.

Gemeente Zuidlaren is the local government for three cities in Holland. The area's abundance of trees, flowers, and two lakes has made it a popular place to live. In creating its corporate identity, designer Erwin Zinger wanted to emphasize the area's park-like setting, traditionally associated with shades of blue and green—a combination of water and earth. Zinger personally didn't like the idea of using blue and green together, but then the client's limited budget forced him to find a one-color option that would graphically represent the area's picturesque environs. Zinger's solution was to print with a combination of blue and green, yielding a teal that visually integrates earth with water, while being a powerful color that differentiates this government letterhead from the norm.

PROJECT	ZUIDLAREN GOVERNMENT IDENTITY SYSTEM
DESIGN FIRM	ERWIN ZINGER GRAPHIC DESIGN
ART DIRECTOR/	
DESIGNER	ERWIN ZINGER
CLIENT	GEMEENTE ZUIDLAREN
	(GOVERNMENT OF ZUIDLAREN)

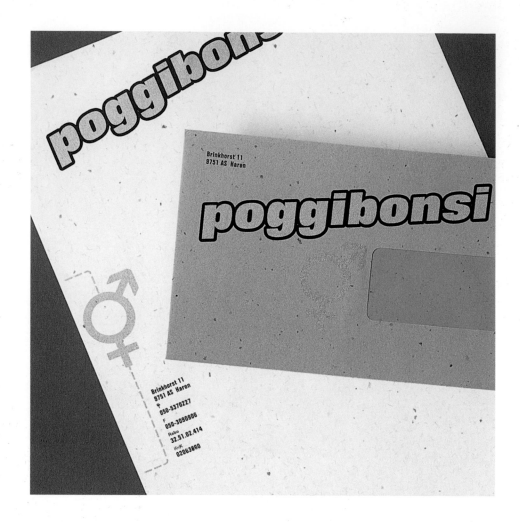

The color palette for Poggibonsi, a fashion retailer that sells business casual clothing for men and women, takes its cue from the city streets. Erwin Zinger employs a myriad of earth-tone colors—olive, tan, cream, ivory, black, and silver—in Poggibonsi's identity system to reflect the current fashion colors worn by the target consumer in The Netherlands. "Because the fashion here in The Netherlands...is mostly black, gray, and brown at this moment, the printing colors black and silver were chosen," explained Zinger. Moreover, Zinger based the palette on the store's very basic interior design. "The different colors of the stationary are an extension of that basic feeling," he said, adding that the identity is so powerful because it is so simple.

PROJECT   POGGIBONSI RETAIL IDENTITY MATERIALS
DESIGN FIRM   ERWIN ZINGER GRAPHIC DESIGN
ART DIRECTOR/
DESIGNER   ERWIN ZINGER
CLIENT   POGGIBONSI

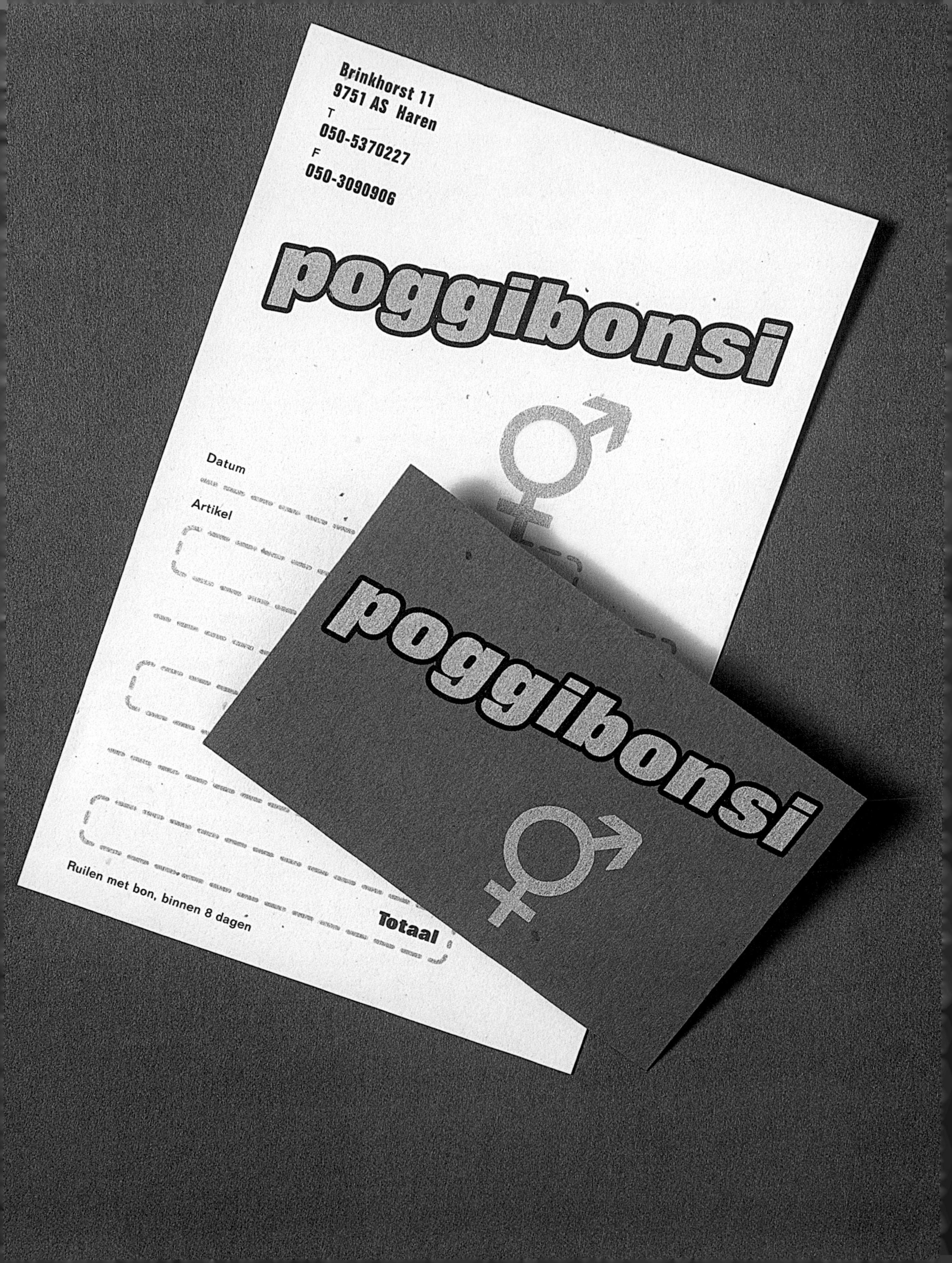
Brinkhorst 11
9751 AS Haren
T
050-5370227
F
050-3090906
poggibonsi
Datum
Artikel
Ruilen met bon, binnen 8 dagen
Totaal
poggibonsi

Spain and Portugal

Deep black, vibrant red, and other strong hues reflect Spain and Portugal's passionate culture and traditions.

As with the flags of many European nations with monarchial traditions, Spain's has evolved from heraldic and amorial banners. The current design, using traditional Spanish royal colors, will sport a different crest of arms emblem for specific occasions. Likewise, Portugal's flag uses a variation of a heraldic coat-of-arms at its center on a field of green and red.

Along with prevailing pan-European color meanings, Spain absorbed the Islamic and North African aesthetic of its longtime Moorish occupiers. Moorish decorative elements fit well into the arid Iberian peninsula; by the time the Moors were driven out of Spain, the country was on its own aesthetic track, distinct from the rest of Europe. The elaborate bas relief work on Spanish palaces, castles, and cathedrals resemble Arab mosques more than any European cathedral. Tiles with blue and green geometric or stylized floral patterns provide soothing visual oases from sun-baked terra cotta roofs and dust-colored stucco walls.

Spain and Portugal interpreted Catholic colors at their most wrathfully pious, establishing black as a power color. Black is also the color of the specially bred bulls used in bullfighting. It is also the color of death.

During the Inquisition, those condemned to be burned were clothed in yellow to display their treason.

Green is the color of racy or sexy jokes; green glass bottles are considered cheap, nasty, and down-market. It is the color of agriculture, particularly the wealth of vineyards in Spain and Portugal.

Red is the color of blood and symbolizes aggression. Bullfighters (matadors) gracefully wield a red cape (muleta) to antagonize a bull. Those who participate in the annual "Running of the Bulls" in Pamplona wear red bandanas. Red is a prominent color in traditional flamenco dresses.

Gray symbolizes strength and is the color of the Rock of Gibraltar, a limestone mass of cliffs and sandy slopes that rises out of the Mediterranean. For years, it was known as the gateway to the Mediterranean and was used as an Allied fortress during World War II.

Purple marks the shade of wine, particularly port, which is produced in the region.

■■ For an international exposition in Seville, the Javier Romero Design Group created a poster that reflects the unique local color of that city. Seville's active nightlife owes much to the heat of Andalusian summer days, and many of the exposition's events began only at dusk, conveyed by the stylized deep blue sky. The particular red-orange color used here is commonly used on local houses and so closely linked to Seville that the Spanish word for it, albero, is as specific as any brand name.

PROJECT   SEVILLE EXPOSITION POSTER
DESIGN FIRM   JAVIER ROMERO DESIGN GROUP

Global Graphics: Colors

■ The warm patina of rich leather is a color unto itself
and when used as a book binding represents a well-
loved, treasured tome. So when the Porto Public Library
organized an exhibition about book covers and invited
Portuguese artists to choose a book and make a cover
using traditional bookbinding, R2 Design chose
Exemplar Fables by Sophia de Mello Breyner
Anderson, and gave it a rich leather cover. "The first
contact with the book is given by the cover. That's our
first image of it," said Lizá Defossez Ramalho. "When
we arrive at the last page, we close the book and we
feel the globality of the title."

PROJECT   EXEMPLAR FABLES BOOK COVER
DESIGN FIRM   R2 DESIGN
ART DIRECTORS/
DESIGNER   LIZÁ DEFOSSEZ RAMALHO, ARTUR REBELO
BOOK BINDER   IMPRENSA PORTUGUESA
CLIENT   BIBLIOTECA MUNICIPAL DO PORTO (PORTO
                 PUBLIC LIBRARY)

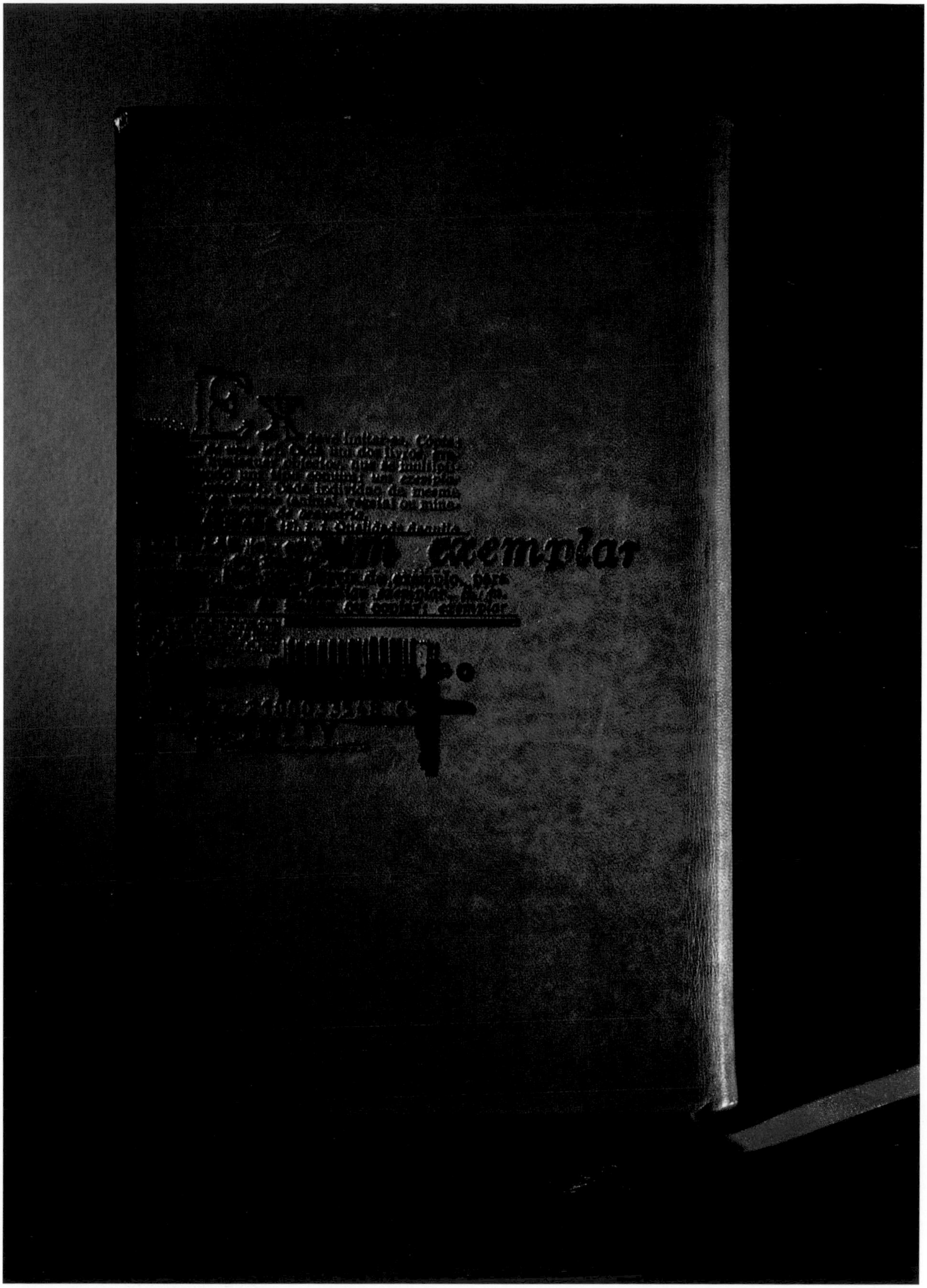

To commemorate a special Port wine for the millennium, Rozès Limitada asked R2 Design to create a bottle dressing and gift pack reflecting the wine's prestige, value, and quality. "The richness of the product suggests 'historical and powerful' colors like black, red, and gold," said Lizá Defossez Ramalho. "We wanted the packaging to reflect the cultural past and history of the Porto wine." To do this, designers used traditional wood packaging; traditional references—including typography that includes the form of a grape—a symbol for wine; and a color palette of black, red, and gold.

PROJECT	ROZÈS MILLENNIUM PORT
DESIGN FIRM	R2 DESIGN
ART DIRECTORS/	
DESIGNERS	LIZÁ DEFOSSEZ RAMALHO, ARTUR REBELO
CLIENT	ROZÈS LIMITADA

■ To promote the production of *Land and Blood*, a theatrical play about crimes that result from envy, R2 Design created a poster with a golden background texture that is stained with a red blood splat. In Portugal as in most countries, red depicts blood, crime, and aggression, while gold is evocative of things of great value, including wealth, jewelry, and the like.

PROJECT	*LAND AND BLOOD* POSTER
DESIGN FIRM	R2 DESIGN
ART DIRECTORS/ DESIGNERS	LIZÁ DEFOSSEZ RAMALHO, ARTUR REBELO
CLIENT	TEATRO BRUTO

Criação Teatro Bruto
ENCARNADO
'98

Encarnado, the title of a play presented by the Teatro
Bruto theatrical group, means red and incarnate in
Portuguese. The climax of the play is a bullfight and its
theme is aggression and the relationship between the
bull and the matador. To graphically convey these concepts, R2 Design used red—an aggressive color and the
color of blood and meat, opposite black, the color of the
bull and the color of death. Together, the colors also
have strong political connotations, according to designers. The color choice had its practical application, too,
as an attention-getter to even casual passers-by. "A
great amount of red in a poster always makes a person
stop," said Lizá Defossez Ramalho.

PROJECT   CRIAÇÃO TEATRO BRUTO ENCARNADO POSTER
DESIGN FIRM   R2 DESIGN
ART DIRECTORS/
DESIGNERS   LIZÁ DEFOSSEZ RAMALHO, ARTUR REBELO
CLIENT   TEATRO BRUTO

■ Vinho Verde is a white wine that is produced in the northwest region of Portugal. Vinho Verde is a young wine that is produced from grapes that are not fully matured, hence its name, which means green wine. To reinforce the wine's origins, João Machado employed a bright leafy green color and the shape of a wine leaf in the logo and letterhead design he created for a firm that organizes guided tours to the farms in the region where the grapes for this unique wine are grown.

PROJECT   ROTA DO VINHO VERDE IDENTITY SYSTEM
DESIGN FIRM   JOÃO MACHADO DESIGN, LDA
ART DIRECTOR/
DESIGNER/
ILLUSTRATOR   JOÃO MACHADO
CLIENT   COMISSÃO DE VITICULTURA DA REGIÃODS
                 VINHOS VERDES (ROTA DO VINHO VERDE)

Global Graphics: Colors

Italy

Colors associated with Italy's vivid history influence modern Italian color usage.

The Italian flag is made up of equal size vertical stripes of green, white, and red.

Many color conventions originated in Roman times, and the preferences of ancient Rome are still visible in modern Italy. The Roman legions used color to distinguish rank and social standing—Roman academics were color coded according to their field of study—and this concept took root in the provinces from Gaul to Britain. Italy didn't go along with the standardized heraldic symbolism codified elsewhere in Europe, but the general idea caught on, and municipal banners, flags, and family crests and colors were used extensively.

Postwar Italy has had a knack for using color in ways that jolt the design world. Olivetti's portable typewriters were startling not just because they were truly portable but because they came in red. The candy colors of the Vespa scooter were initially as startling as the vehicle's redefinition of urban transportation.

Here, along with lingering hues redolent of the glory that was Rome, are some uniquely Italian color associations.

Red was the color of Mars, god of war; the color of light; often used in interiors. It was also a token of a widow's fidelity to her late husband. Aging Romans preferred the red-orange of henna to gray hair. There is a national preference for red apples over green. When used in combination with green and white, it denotes the country itself, comprising the colors of the Italian flag, thanks in part to the abundance of pizza parlors and Italian restaurants that use these colors in their own color schemes.

Dark blue was the Roman color of mourning. The concept of a bluestocking—high brow, imperious, judgmental—stems from the Venetian convention of color-coding the hosiery of its social strata.

Purple was the color of emperors and gods; always used for high-ranking officials, victorious generals, and royalty, as the Empire expanded purple became more exclusively the property of nobility, signifying the emperor's personification of the god Jupiter. At various points in Roman history the unauthorized use—even possession—of purple clothing by anyone not eligible was severely punished.

Gold togas were worn by victorious generals. Rich shades of dark gold are associated with Italian 18 karat jewelry as seen in the busy shops that line Florence's Ponte Vecchio, a city known for its goldsmithing. Venice's Ca' d' Oro (house of gold) is the home of priceless museum treasures.

Venice's world-famous gondolas are black.

Silver, like gold, is also an Italian staple. Artisan silver filigree jewelry and handmade objects are highly coveted.

Jupiter's chariot was drawn by white horses; a white horse became symbolic of its rider's greatness and elevated status. White bulls were sacrificed to Jupiter. Women of high virtue wore white.

In addition to its association with the earth, particularly in the agricultural regions, brown is associated with the rich patina of fine Italian leather goods that are highly valued throughout the world.

Roman Catholic and Christian Colors

Of the colors associated with Christian theology (and the Catholic church in particular), few are mentioned in scripture. Most of these associations evolved over centuries, absorbing, appropriating, and incorporating color symbolism from Roman traditions, pagan religions, and artistic convention prompted by the availability or cost of materials. Western art through the Renaissance—painting in particular—is essentially an illustrated history of the growing power of the Roman Catholic Church.

Debate raged throughout the Middle Ages over which color garments monks should wear. The choices were white for purity, brown for earthiness, or black for humility. No overall resolution was reached, and individual orders chose according to their own philosophy. Five colors are recognized for ecclesiastical uses: white, red, green, purple, and black. One of these five colors will occupy the main portion of a vestment; borders and ornamental decoration can be added, and the lining is often yellow or gold.

Red is the traditional color of Christ's robes and, along with purple, martyrdom in general. As the power of the church grew and that of the Roman Empire diminished, the Christian symbolism of red displaced the divine status of purple that had been the color of Roman emperors and gods. Scarlet symbolizes charity, and has an overall positive link to good works and Christ-like piety. Red and black together are often used to describe the apocalypse.

Portraying the traitorous disciple Judas in yellow robes was a medieval artistic convention with no basis in scripture; but because Christ was often portrayed in red and the Virgin Mary in blue, having Judas wear yellow was a convenient way to balance the primary color scheme. So yellow gained its reputation as the color of cowardice, treachery, and shame. Still, yellow is one of a small handful of colors acceptable for use as a border on Catholic vestments. Yellow is also routinely used as a stand-in for gold. Together with its complement purple, yellow is emblematic of Easter.

Blue is the color of hope, heaven, purity, and virtue. Blue is used in some dioceses in Spain for masses celebrating the Immaculate Conception. Blue became the favored color for representing the Virgin Mary's robe in the early Renaissance.

Green is the color of faith, immortality, and contemplation; symbolic of rebirth (resurrection) and eternal life. It is the color of baptism. Priests may wear green vestments after epiphany, as a symbol of the birth of a new year.

Brown is the color of the robes of the Reformed order of the Franciscans (the un-Reformed wear gray). Brown symbolizes penitence, renunciation of earthly things, and humility. Carmelites wear white over brown.

Commissions for Renaissance paintings included a budget for materials and sometimes stipulated whether a particularly expensive substance was to be supplied by the painter or the patron. A painting's size and even composition could be determined by its materials fee; artists could view the work of a rival and know immediately whether he had been paid handsomely or had labored on the cheap. The pragmatic Leonardo da Vinci circumvented budget constraints on his use of expensive lapis lazuli by building up areas of that color with a less expensive blue paint, then applied the precious stuff only to the top layer where it could be seen to best effect.

116 · 117

Purple conveys endurance of suffering; martyrs are often represented wearing purple. Rosaries are often made of amethyst. Purple also symbolizes the blending of the blue of the spirit and the red of martyrs' blood.

Used to signify divinity, as haloes around holy figures—Christs, the Madonna, saints, and martyrs. Gold-plated ritual implements, like the chalice, are part of church services; gold also adorns the vestments of priests. Gold is used extensively in the decoration of church interiors, where it serves as an imposing show of power and wealth, linked to things divine. Paradoxically, gold is also used as a sign of greed and avarice in worldly matters—a temptation away from God.

The color for death and mourning is black, according to Christian conventions. It is also the color of penitence, humility, and asceticism, making it a common color for the garments worn by priests, monks, and nuns. Orders that wear black are Benedictines, Augustinians, Jesuits; Dominicans wear black over white.

The color of purity, whether literal or symbolic virginity; the clouds of heaven; robes of apostles; white of sheep; and the second most popular color for representations of Christ's robes (a red sash may be slung over his shoulder). A white dove, like that released by Noah at the end of the Great Flood, is a symbol of peace and heavenly presence. White and gold together represent Christmas and Easter, and may be worn by the priest presiding over Mass on those days. White is the color of Cistercians, the Order of the Holy Cross, and the reformed branch of the Benedictines.

Italian city states of the Middle Ages and the Renaissance used a system of banners and crests comparable to the heraldic symbolism in northern Europe. The city colors of Florence and its fleur-de-lis symbol are employed here for an international student organization's event held in that city.

PROJECT   STUDENT ORGANIZATION LOGO
DESIGN FIRM   SWIETER DESIGN US

118 · 119

Various shades of blue and blue-green are representative of the sea and summer breezes in Italy; moreover, the cool hues conjure up a pleasant sensation of freshness, according to Gianluigi Tobanelli, who employed these colors when creating the packaging for Fria moist towelettes. The upscale product is available in two materials—pure cellulose and cotton—at selected Italian perfumeries and pharmacies. In addition to the blue-green color palette, the designer used gold to underline the high quality of the product. "Great attention has been given to the packaging itself as well as its color," said Tobanelli. "Our aim was to communicate the refreshing power of the moist towelette and the high quality of the materials used to the Italian consumer."

PROJECT	FRIA MOIST TOWELETTE PACKAGING
DESIGN FIRM	STUDIO GT & P
ART DIRECTOR	GIANLUIGI TOBANELLI
CLIENT	DIVA INTERNATIONAL S.R.L.

Eastern Europe

Eastern Europe is a jumble of countries and unresolved territorial disputes. Nearly all of these countries have been conquered by, aligned with, or annexed to one or another neighbor on a regular basis since the Renaissance. Since the end of the Soviet Union, former Soviet bloc countries have been rediscovering, restoring, and reinventing their individual identities.

This region is far from being a uniformly grim industrialized landscape. There are, of course, factories and industrial centers as gritty as any, and plenty of worker housing; but much of Eastern Europe is rural, with vast tracts of farmland, and towns and villages that look like storybook illustrations.

The good news about designing for Eastern Europe is that, for the most part, the color conventions of Western Europe apply. The bad news is that former national identities are not always useful or informative. A helpful starting point is to determine the cultural forces that have most shaped each country; were Roman Catholicism, the Greek Orthodox church or Protestantism the religion of choice? Was Byzantine art a factor? With which empire (Ottoman, Austro-Hungarian, Holy Roman) was the country aligned with or annexed to?

Estonia and Latvia have historic ties to Scandinavia, and Lithuania was part of the Russian Empire long before the Soviet Union. Poland is fervently Roman Catholic, and has long-standing cultural links to France. Hungary, a key part of the Austro-Hungarian Empire, has a history of stern Lutheranism and Calvinism, and a reputation for a spare, modern aesthetic. Slovakia is culturally closer to Hungary than to its former partner the Czech Republic, which in turn shares more in common with its German and Austrian neighbors.

Although few folk traditions are practiced today, their presence is still evident. The exteriors of churches in Romania are painted with brightly colored frescoes (the interiors, by contrast, are simple and spare). In the Transylvanian region of Hungary, a multi-colored country cottage with a blue stripe along the ground level indicates that an unmarried woman resides there. There are traces of gypsy folklore and superstition here and there; akin to the Greek custom (and perhaps even learned from Greece), gypsies paint doorways blue to keep away evil spirits.

Another important consideration is how much exposure to Western European culture each country experienced during the Cold War. There has been a lively art scene in the East for decades; their circus posters, political art, theater, and animation are much admired in the West.

■ Columbia Records asked Germany's Braue Design to create an image and CD packaging for Dino Raffelos, a songwriter from Greece. The client wanted a design that would reflect the Greek artist's emotionally driven ballads. To meet the objective, Marçel Robbers designed the CD insert with a palette of warm, rich browns. Other elements of Greek culture, including the statuary, added the finishing touch to the design. All totalled, the elements combine to evoke the emotional, passionate nature of the songwriter and the Greek culture.

PROJECT	DINO RAFFAELOS CD AMIGOS PARA SIEMPRÉ
DESIGN FIRM	BRAUE DESIGN
ART DIRECTOR/ DESIGNER	MARÇEL ROBBERS
CLIENT	COLUMBIA RECORDS

Greece

Many conventional color meanings originated in ancient Greece culture.

True to its geography, the Greek flag is blue and white.

It is the blue of the sea and the white of the houses on Aegean islands that spring immediately to mind in regards to Greece. Whitewashed houses to reflect the sunlight; window frames, shutters, and doors are often painted green or blue. The blue is sometimes meant to ward off the evil eye, but is a common convention regardless of its intent. Greece straddles southern and eastern Europe, and, as the center of Eastern Orthodox religion, Byzantine art has been the biggest and most consistent influence on Greek color use. Many conventional color meanings began in ancient Greece; the country pretty much missed out on the Renaissance and the pervasive influence of the Roman Catholic Church.

Red is the color of love. Dionysus, the god of wine, was portrayed with a reddened face; red is the color of the festival of wine. Red also signifies autumn, and the red poppy was the sacred flower of Ceres, goddess of the harvest. The shields and tunics of Spartan warriors were red, perhaps the first military uniform. Those reciting the Iliad wore red, the color of sacrifice.

Yellow stands for spring, and was the color of the goddess Artemis. Amber was the color of official buildings of the fascist occupiers of Greece before and during the Second World War, and is not popular these days, especially in architecture.

Green is the color-symbol for water and the earth. An emerald on the breastplate of the goddess Athena signified her divinity and wisdom.

The word purple comes from the Greek porphura, a species of shellfish from which the dye, Tyrain Purple is made. It is used to dye royal cloaks and carpets and was used as a remedy for boils and ulcers; it worked because of its high calcium oxide content. In a fit of hubris, Agamemnon broke the rule about reserving purple carpet for use only by the gods, and had one rolled out for him upon a triumphant return from battle; he was subsequently stabbed by his wife.

Black was the color symbol for winter in antiquity.

Commonwealth of Independent States

Georgia, Armenia, Azerbzizan, Turkmenistan, Tajikistan, Uzbekistan, Krygtan, Kazakstan, Russia

Not surprisingly, red is an important color in the flags of the Commonwealth of Independent States, which includes Russia. Armenia, however, differs from the rest with its band of orange (along with blue and red).

In Moscow today you are more likely to see a red star on a bottle of San Pellegrino Water or Heineken Beer than on tanks trundling past a reviewing stand filled with applauding apperatchiks. A more European color scheme has replaced the region's historical use of red.

Western ways have been commonplace in Russia since the 18th century, when French culture was widely emulated - French was even the language of choice among the upper class of Imperial Russian society. Pan-European color uses and conventions are the rule today; and imported items are much more desirable than anything domestic. Therefore, there is no advantage in trying to make something foreign look Russian.

Russia never fully let go of a Byzantine aesthetic, and this is the one big distinction between it and the rest of Europe. While the Renaissance was in full swing to the south, Russian icon painting was reaching its zenith. The Byzantine style is characterized by religious subject matter, formal compositions of stylized figures, symbolic use of color (Virgin Mary in blue, etc.), and gold, gold, and more gold. The gold leaf provides a flat, planeless, depth of field-defying background and a luminous, heavenly quality. The intent was to make the painting virtually glow in even dim light.

The Hermitage in St. Petersburg houses one of the finest art collections in the world, but the building itself is almost too much; gilded to its baroque rafters, it is like a Fabergé egg expanded to the size of Versailles. Decoration for the Russian aristocracy was always over the top. The resurgence of open religious worship has revived icon painting on a grand scale. At Easter, newly created banners portraying Christ and his disciples in the traditional Byzantine style hang in Red Square, where pictures of Stalin once rippled in the breeze.

Russian art kept pace with the prevailing European styles and is stylistically indistinguishable from its 19th century French contemporaries. Pre-Soviet 20th century Russian art and decor is typified by the exotic set and costume designs of the Ballets Russes, which inspired such French fashion designers as Paul Poirot. The Constructivist movement of the 1920s was briefly at the avant-garde of the international art scene and remains an enormous influence worldwide; but by the 1930s Stalin decreed that Socialist-Realist art was of better service to the state, and from then on things were dominated by heroically scaled works extolling collectivist values.

RED SCARE

Not long after the fall of the Soviet Union, a newly formed Moscow advertising agency landed the Coca-Cola account for the Russian market. The agency's senior partners, in their zeal to avoid any link to recently departed Soviet iconography, were in the midst of choosing a color with which to replace Coke's traditional red background. Green was a frontrunner until an American college student interning with them explained that red was the signature color of the beverage and that the company would not probably not look kindly on its being changed.

Red is, of course, shorthand for communist and revolution; but it also conveys the myriad of meanings it has elsewhere in Europe. Red and yellow are traditional Russian wedding colors, and a red neon M denotes Metro (subway) entrances in both Moscow and St. Petersburg. Red Square gets its name not from the color of the Kremlin or the onion-domed St. Basil's cathedral—although they are both built of red brick—or from any Bolshevik reference; rather, the Russian word for beautiful is pronounced the same as the English word red.

Moldova is a leading producer of sunflowers. Yellow is also a traditional Russian wedding color.

Decoration for the Russian aristocracy always over utilized gold: the more gold the better. The official coat of arms of Ukraine is a gold trident on an azure background.

The logo for the Astro Space Center in Moscow is a stylized blue starburst with a small red dot next to it. In religion, blue is associated with the Virgin Mary. This style of painting was characterized in part by symbolic use of color. Blue symbolized hope, heaven, purity, and virtue. Pale blue symbolized peace and serenity.

The repousse triptych of the Khakhuli Virgin, known as the Khakhuli icon, was created sometime between the eight and twelfth centuries and is now housed in the Georgian State Museum of Fine Art. The triptych's side panels are encased in repousse silverwork, and silver is also used elsewhere on this important symbol of Georgia.

Orange is found in the Armenian flag.

In a poster for a festival of Russian theatrical works being performed in New York, the colors of these silhouette depicitions of the onion domes of St. Basel's Cathedral in Moscow—which match the building's actual colors—helps to reinforce their immediate recognition.

PROJECT   **THE MOSCOW ARTS FESTIVAL ON BROADWAY POSTER**

Turkey

Turkey's flag is red and white, but the city of Istanbul has its own flag that's of a slightly different hue: a pinkish raspberry color.

Deep turquoise and warm reds typify the Turkey's major color influences

Turkey is a mix of ancient civilizations—including the Romans, Ottomans, Persians, and Macedonians—that date back to 9000 BC and whose influence is still apparent. At the same time it is a thoroughly modern country, complete with a younger generation with a great fondness for Levis. While agriculture is still a major moneymaker, technology and Western influences threaten the country's ties with its past. Some things, like landscape, never really change, though, so there are some reliable sources of local color. The Turkish landscape is so varied—you can find snow-capped mountains, highlands dotted with wildflowers in spring, rich, green valleys, and barren bedrock that changes from gold to violet to gray, depending on the sun. Turkey is also known for its ornamental flowers, not least of which is the tulip. The interest in these ornamental flowers grew to such an extent that the seventeenth-century in Turkey is known as the Tulip age.

The word turquoise is French for "Turkish stone." Greatly admired throughout the Middle East, it was also believed to have preventative and healing medicinal powers. That turquoise can deteriorate when touched reinforced the belief that it could detect illness. It was also believed capable of warding off the evil eye; people used it in charms and amulets to protect themselves and their livestock. Blue and turquoise were expensive colors to produce, so their use in art (frescoes especially) indicated wealth and/or ingenuity.

Red is the predominant color of Turkey's kilim rugs, which also may include other warm colors such as yellow, orange, beige, and black. Red can also signify cherries, which—along with apricots, almonds, and figs—originated in Turkey.

Along with turquoise, light and dark blue, and black, purple, white, and gold can be found in the tiles of zoomorphic, floral, geometric, arabesque patterns that are part of the Turkish aesthetic. In parts of Turkey, barren bedrock changes color with the sun from gold to violet to gray.

Pink flamingos may not be the first birds to come to mind when thinking of Turkey, but they actually nest in the river valleys of the Aegean and the Mediterranean and spend their winters inland in the salt-water lakes.

Bessi Karavil, a designer based in Milan, Italy, created this packaging for a children's clothing store in Istanbul. Karavil kept the look light, choosing to use a peachy-tan color palette as the base accented with brown. The wallpaper that decorates Dodo Junior shops was the inspiration for the logo design and the color choice.

PROJECT   DODO JUNIOR IDENTITY SYSTEM
DESIGN FIRM   STUDIO KARAVIL
ART DIRECTOR/
DESIGNER   BESSI KARAVIL
PRINTER   NAZ ETIKET

Balkans and Slavic States

Albania, Madeconia, Bulgaria, Romania, Bosnia, Herzegovina, Croatia, Hungary, Slovakia, Czech Republic, Ukraine, Moldova, Poland, Belarus, Lithuania, Latvia, Estonia

ESTONIA

HUNGARY

ROMANIA

126 · 127

Red dominates the flags in this part of the world, with Estonia as a notable exception—it's blue, black, and white.

The influence of folklore results in this region's usage of bright colors and combinations

Estonia and Latvia have historic ties to Scandinavia, and Lithuania was part of the Russian Empire long before the Soviet Union. Poland is fervently Roman Catholic, and has long-standing cultural links to France. Hungary, a key part of the Austro-Hungarian Empire, has a history of stern Lutheranism and Calvinism, and a reputation for a spare, modernist aesthetic. Slovakia is culturally closer to Hungary than to its former partner, the Czech Republic, which in turn shares more in common with its German and Austrian neighbors.

Although few folk traditions are practiced today, their presence is still evident. The exteriors of churches in Romania are painted with brightly colored frescoes (the interiors, by contrast, are simple and spare). In the Transylvanian region of Hungary, a multi-colored country cottage with a blue stripe along the ground level indicates that an unmarried woman resides there. There are traces of gypsy folklore and superstition here and there; akin to the Greek custom (and perhaps even learned from Greece), gypsies paint doorways blue to keep away evil spirits.

Red is a major component of the flags of Lithuania and Latvia. It is thought to have medicinal properties: red wool was used to relieve fevers in Macedonia.

Blue was commonly used in frescoes decorating churches.

The state emblem of Lithuania features a white knight on a white horse against a red background. White clothing was traditionally a symbol of neatness, diligence, and intelligence. White linen was believed to have magic powers.

In the Lithuanian folktale "Egle, Queen of the Serpents," the main character leaves her family and meets a handsome young man on a beach who takes her to an amber palace under the sea. Amber is also a natural resource of Latvia.

Green forests cover 50 percent of Latvia, with nearly 67 percent of them composed of pine.

■ ■ The red and blue of the logo for Croatia reflects
colors often found in the flags of the region.

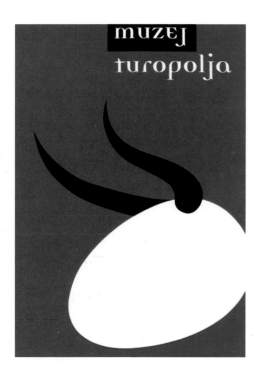

■ ■ The green and the black on this creation are not only dramatic, but the green shade reflects the color of the forests found all over the region.

PROJECT	**MUZEJ TUROPOLJA**
DESIGN FIRM	**LIKOVNI STUDIO D.O.O.**
DESIGNER	**MRCIC & JAKSIC**
CLIENT	**MUZEJ TUROPOLJA**

Middle East

The Middle East is the birthplace of three major world religions and is the cradle of Western—perhaps world—civilization. Color plays a significant role in the rituals, ceremonies and decoration of Judaism, Islam and Christianity, but there are few if any directives from these religions regarding secular color use. When designing for the Holy Land, it is political, rather than religious, color-related faux pas one must watch for.

National flags, while not themselves objects of reverence, may include important symbols or scripture from the Koran. Verify that colors you wish to use do not appear on the flag or banner of enemy countries or internal rebel movements. Some countries have lingering ill feelings toward the European powers that once had colonial holdings in the region. There is admiration and a market for French products in Morocco, for instance, but in neighboring Algeria there is still bitter hostility (and sometimes violence) aimed at the French.

Red, green, white, and black together are the colors of the Pan-Arab movement, and appear on the flags of several Islamic countries. The second most common color combination is turquoise, blue, and gold with green and red. These colors are seen in architecture and mosaics, particularly on mosques.

Long-time denizens of the Middle East are the Bedouins. Described as dressing "as somberly as a British banker," the nomadic Bedouins may have been one of the first groups to opt for basic black as everyday wear. Their two main decorative traditions are weaving and silverwork. Displays of color are reserved for the pillows and wall hangings inside their tents. Typical colors for Bedouin woven goods include the natural color of the sheep or goat's coat, along with deep red, indigo, green, orange, and mustard. From a distance, the traditional Bedouin tent — beit al-sha'r or house of hair—looks black but is actually an earthy charcoal gray, with streaks of dark brown created by the mingling of different shades of the loosely woven wool. Inside, a colorful curtain acts as a wall, separating the mens' and womens' sections.

Jewelry is the property of women. Bedouin jewelry tends to be large and elaborate, and is intended as both decoration and a show of wealth. Oddly, Bedouins have no silversmithing tradition themselves, relying instead upon artisans in settlements that they pass. Silversmiths with a steady Bedouin clientele created similar designs in different grades of silver, allowing even humble families to adorn their women in style. Pieces are studded with amber, coral, agate, carnelian, pearls, or turquoise. Surfaces are embossed with calligraphic inscriptions from the Koran or curvilinear, abstract designs. A stack of bracelets is worn daily, and for special occasions, a woman might wear every piece of her jewelry that she can fit on at once, including necklaces and headdresses. She may also wear all of her finger rings at the same time, as a show that she won't be doing any cooking.

Israel

Israel's palette reflects its various immigrant cultural influences.

The Israeli flag features a blue Star of David which sits between two horizontal blue stripes on a field of white.

JEWISH RITE COLORS

Priests of the temple in old Jerusalem wore a breastplate decorated with twelve stones each representing the tribes of Israel: sardonyx, topaz, emerald, carbuncle, jasper, sapphire, ligure, amethyst, agate, chrysolite, onyx, and beryl. This range of colors symbolically embodied aspects of God, humanity, and life. Red, blue, purple, and white are the divine colors of Judaism.

A nation of immigrants, Israel has absorbed aspects of almost every other culture on earth. Traditional, ritual, and ceremonial colors specific to the Jewish religion are, of course, important. So are the customs and beliefs of the secular societies from which contemporary Israelis have come. European and American mass culture are quite familiar here, more so than elsewhere in the region, and despite the clout of religious hard-liners, there is a healthy, secular side of daily life. There are few color taboos, but one should be careful to avoid color combinations associated with neighboring countries that are hostile to the state of Israel. The pan-Arab colors of green, red, black, and white together are probably best avoided.

In the Kabalah, red refers to love, sacrifice, and sin. Scarlet is fire. Red also means spilled blood, anger, and hatred; it also conveys strength.

Amber was the color described to be emanating from god and the area surrounding him on more than one occasion of a heavenly visitation to earth.

Blue is the color of the Lord. In Exodus there is a description of the seventy elders who, when they see the God of Israel, say that under his feet was "a paved work of sapphire stone." Blue symbolizes glory in the Kabalah. God commanded Moses to have the Jews add blue fringes to the borders of their clothing to convey glory; and blue is the color of the Israeli flag.

In the Jewish color coding of the elements of nature, purple represents the sea, probably because the color was produced from shellfish. Purple is also a color of divinity.

As in other religions, gold is somewhat paradoxical; it appears often in the decoration of temples and fine objects, but is warned against as an object of desire and worship.

White signifies earth in the elements of nature. In the Kabalah, white indicates mercy and peace. This may be due to white hair being equated with age and wisdom; also someone too old to be in army and therefore, peaceable. White signifies purity and joy.

Egypt

Color use in Egypt today is a mix of the ancient and the modern.

The red, white, and black striped Egyptian flag features three of the colors of pan-Arab unity, with an eagle—symbol of the Moslem ruler Saladin—in the center.

Along with the pyramids and the Sphinx, the ancient Egyptians left a legacy of color therapy and brilliant cosmetics. Color figured in many aspects of life in the time of the pharaohs, and conventional color use in Egypt today is a juxtaposition of the ancient and the up-to-the-minute.

Red and white striped Bedouin rugs from the northern coast are seen throughout the country. In Ancient Egypt, Shu, the god who separated the earth from the sky was red, and red stones were used in the treatments of diseases and for protection from fire and lightning. Red oxen and even redheaded youths were sacrificed to ensure a good harvest in ancient Egypt. Red post boxes are for regular domestic mail.

Bees were symbols of the lower pharaoh, the soul, and the sun; the combination of gold (or yellow) and black, especially stripes, was significant, and retains resonance. Hek, the ancient god of magic, had yellow skin. Yellow stones were believed to bring happiness and prosperity.

Ancient Egyptian decoration favored a chalky—almost Wedgwood—blue for backgrounds. Pharoanic priests adorned their ceremonial breastplates with blue, symbolizing truth and justice. The ancient god of life and reproduction was blue, and blue and violet stones were associated with virtue and faith. Egyptians have always been fond of blue, in the form of lapis lazuli, turquoise or Egyptian faience. Post boxes for overseas airmail are blue.

Rugs made in the Sinai feature green and orange diamond patterns. In the ancient Middle Kingdom, certain colors were held to be magical and medicinal: Green stones were believed to promote fertility and were connected with rain, vegetation, and strength. Post boxes are green for Cairo mail and express delivery within Cairo.

Egyptian taxicabs have orange license plates.

Gold is the most coveted and frequently used metal for jewelry today, but silver was once the metal of choice. Items too large to be affordably made of gold are still made of silver. Shops that sell gold plate are known by the large gilded camel sign or statue in the window.

Black cats were revered by ancient Egyptians, and held to be lucky and even sacred. Seth, deity of the north, of evil, and of darkness was represented as black.

Egyptian cotton is the finest in the world, and the raw color of the stuff evokes quality. Thought to come from heaven, white stones are supposed to have special power, particularly to ward off the Evil Eye. White signified Osiris and purity, as well as symbolizing Horus, god of the passage of time.

Ancient Egyptian Colors

Many long-standing color uses originated in ancient Egypt, including the tradition of marking important calendar days and events in red. Cleopatra's favorite makeup colors can be found at the cosmetics counter of any 20th century department store; in her time, they were created from finely powdered minerals like anthracite and lapis lazuli. The Queen of the Nile favored black eyebrows and eyelashes, dark blue and green eye shadow. There was a practical aspect to this heavy eye makeup, which reflected the relentless Egyptian sun and protected the eyes. Her contemporaries lined their eyes in black and gray, painted their nipples gold, and accented the veins on their temples and breasts with blue. Even men would paint the palms of their hands and bottoms of their feet in reddish orange henna. Yellow was used to lighten skin tones.

The Egyptians (and the Sumerians who preceded them) used gems and colorful stones and shells for religious and medicinal purposes as well as cosmetic purposes. Treatments for various ailments specified substances of particular colors. Egyptians assigned divine associations to the water's color changes during the annual flood cycle of the Nile. Red was the blood of Osiris, shed to rejuvenate the land; white the color of the god Hapi flowing down from the stars; green the color of spring vegetation and planting, black the color of gestation. Statues of the goddess Isis were painted different colors to mark different occasions and needs: green for nature; black for death, corruption and degeneration; red for sunrise. White, yellow and red signify the trinity of sunrise, day, and dusk.

Morocco

The Moroccan flag features a green star diagram on a field of red.

A riot of exotic colors typifies Morocco's color scheme—and its famous marketplaces.

Just a short swim across the Straits of Gibraltar from Spain, Morocco shares a similar climate and landscape and once occupied Spain; France, in turn, occupied Morocco from 1912 to 1956. Still, Morocco has had more of a cultural and aesthetic effect on its visitors than the other way around. Artist Henri Matisse got a lot of mileage out of his two trips to Tangiers, and the body of paintings inspired by those visits is worth a look for anyone designing for the Moroccan marketplace. The painting Cafe Marocain (1912), in particular, with its blue-green background and spots of white and gold, framed by a gold border, displays color combinations widely associated with the country.

Henna is used for many things in Morocco, often to temporarily dye skin for ceremonial decoration; the hands of wedding guests are often hennaed in ornate patterns. The markets of Marrakech are full of henna leaves, powders, dyes, and the products made from them.

Petit-cabs, which can only take fares within cities, are usually sub-compact European cars painted crimson (cars for hire for longer trips tend to be mid-size Mercedes). Ftouh are vivid red and white striped wraps worn by women from the Jibali tribes. They are not symbolically meaningful, but are unique to Morocco and seen and worn throughout the country.

Moroccan post boxes are yellow. Mail service is slow and unreliable, so it doesn't carry a very positive implication, but, as no one expects the mail service to be efficient, it isn't a big negative, either. For men, canary yellow leather slippers are considered the most dignified of the many available colors. A stretch of Morocco's Atlantic coast is known as the Yellow Coast because of the yellowish clay found there. When used for pottery, this clay is often decorated with distinctive black curvilinear designs and a greenish-blue glaze, nicknamed turquoise by the French.

The blue pottery made in the city of Fez and known as Fakhari is of a color known as Bleu de Fez. Almost turquoise, it is often—erroneously—called by that name. Bleu de Fez pottery designs strictly follows the Islamic prohibition of depicting the natural world, and instead feature geometric non-representational designs. A blue spot was once painted behind the ear of a bridegroom to ward off evil. Blue doors and doorways are common; there is no particular significance to it besides offering a welcome, cool appearance in the harsh sunlight.

Green is not used much in textiles, but is seen mostly in the elaborate tilework of buildings, particularly mosques.

Gold is used a lot. Aside from its decorative purposes, gold jewelry is believed to have mystical powers. A gold pendant in the shape of a hand wards off the evil eye; wedding guests wear gold belts, recalling the days when a gold belt was part of the price of buying a bride from her family.

White is worn on Fridays and on special occasions.

Berber silver work and precious stones are one of the country's characteristic crafts. It tends to be chunky and large, oversized for its purposes—earrings and brooches are the size of doorknobs. Silver and brass household items are a fine craft in Morocco, and even daily items like serving trays and teapots are elegantly executed.

Saudi Arabia

Colors associated with Islam and Muslim culture are prevalent in this holy land.

On the flag is a green field and a sword and the words in Arabic script: "There is no God but Allah, and Mohammed is the Prophet of Allah."

Saudi Arabia is the home of Mecca, birthplace of Mohammed, and a sacred place of pilgrimage for all Moslems. The country does billions of dollars worth of oil business with nearly every other nation on earth, so there is great familiarity with foreign things and ways; European and American, in particular. A common mistake made by those introducing things into the Saudi marketplace is to treat Arabic script as just another design element. In and of itself, this is offensive; to top it off, the script is often stylized to the point of distorting it into gibberish. In Arabic writing, an entire word or concept may be contained within a single written character, and even subtle differences can alter the meaning.

Saudi males wear the traditional thobe, a wool robe that, in its uniformity, is meant to express equality. In hot weather a white thobe is worn; in cooler weather, one of black. On special occasions, a long white, brown, or black cloak trimmed in gold is worn over the thobe. The traditional headdress is white or red and white checked, with a black cord that holds it in place. Headdress color is of no particular significance.

Stones of red, whether agate, carnelian, garnet, or coral are the favorite of Bedouin jewelers (and wearers). Agate is believed to make the wearer more personable; coral induces wisdom; garnet alleviates bleeding and inflammation.

Sapphires are symbols of chastity; turquoise is believed to reflect the wearer's mood, glowing when they are happy, losing its luster when they are sad.

Along with its Holy Islamic associations, green is a sign of prestige in a totally secular way; a lawn or many plants on the property are reserved for the wealthy in this arid environment. Green stones are traditionally believed to ward off sickness of various kinds.

Saudi women wear gold jewelry, but most Saudi men follow the Islamic dictate against adorning themselves with gold. Objects made of and plated with gold are quite popular.

A black silk covering—the Kiswa—embroidered in gold and silver with Koranic text, is kept over the Kaaba (the precise spot Moslems face when praying), at Mecca. In addition, within the Kaaba is the sacred Black Stone (al-Hajar al-Aswad). Saudi women wear a large black cloak called an abayah, a scarf over their head, and a full face veil when out in public. It is common, however, for Saudi women to have fashionable and very colorful clothing underneath their abayah.

Pilgrims go to holy places dressed in an unseamed length of white cloth girded around the waist with a cord, with another length of cloth draped over the left shoulder. Diamonds are hugely popular in Saudi Arabia for both men and women.

A huge silver frame protects the Kaaba, the sacred Black Stone at Mecca.

Islamic Colors

Islam is the preeminent social and religious force in the Middle East. Its influence stretches from Pakistan in Central Asia to Morocco on the Atlantic coast of North Africa. There are many references to color in the Koran but few about its meaning or use; most of those associations come from Islamic poetry which, while influential, is not sacred. The two most significant colors are green, the color of the robe of the prophet Mohammed, and blue, for water, the sky and the heavens.

The Koran prohibits the representation of human or animal figures in art, so mosque decor is all non-figurative calligraphic embellishment: tiles, mosaics, and even textured patterns etched into the walls. The use of mosaic is extensive in Islam; mosques are meant to be spiritual oases that "refresh the soul and engage the heart" and the architectural emphasis on the light and light-enhancing tesserae of mosaics was intended to inspired both delight and awe.

Along with its universal connection to blood, in Islam a red rose is symbolic of Allah's perfect beauty. Red is the official color of the Sharifs (protectors) of Mecca.

Often used with green tiles in mosques and for decorative flourishes, the positive associations of blue come from allegories made by Islamic poets, who likened personal union with God to the submersion of one drop of water into the ocean. More prosaically, water is a precious and important commodity in this arid region.

Because green is the color of Mohammed's robes, it is the color of those of perfect faith. Pilgrims to Mecca wear a green headdress, and in Islamic theology heaven is described as a lush garden. Mosques feature green tilework inside and out (some modern mosques illuminate their exteriors at night with green lights). On a more secular plane, green means the fecundity of the earth. The flags of many Islamic countries prominently feature green--Libya's flag, for example, is simply a banner of green. The sacredness of the color depends upon whether Sunni or Shiite Moslems rule. Of the two, Shiite is more fundamentalist and less open to secularism.

There are contradictory attitudes about gold in the Moslem world. There is no ban on its use for decorative purposes, but gold is denounced as a trigger of greed and a prompter evil doings. Gold jewelry is not supposed to be worn by men (although it is not unheard of), but women may adorn themselves lavishly.

Believed to be the color that conceals the radiant beauty of divine truth. The robes that Moslem women wear are of black, carrying forward the notion of black covering or containing beauty.

138 · 139

■ ■ The decorative flourishes of green and blue tiles in this mosque have positive allegoric associations with the precious resource water, and union with Mohammed.

Africa

There is no single, unifying pan-African aesthetic, but there are commonalities and consistent themes throughout the continent. Whether something is damp or dry, smooth or wrinkled is most important; light or dark is noted next; only after these considerations is color significant. In some societies smooth, lustrous surfaces, echoing healthy skin, are prized; in others that have a tradition of scarification, elaborate and ornately carved objects are the standard of beauty. A common theme is the use of repetitive linear designs carved into stone walls, wooden doors, and furniture, or printed on textiles. Hatching, concentric circles, and curvy waving lines show up engraved onto ornate wooden doors of houses in the forest lands of West Africa, and printed on the Pakhamani cloths of the South. In many African societies, artisans were nearly on a par with shamans for conveying magic and religious meaning through their work. The inferred meanings of a piece of art are considered more important than its surface beauty. Clarity of form and detail, complexity, symmetry, and balance of composition are valued, and mastery of craft, whether in wood or metal sculpture, decorative carving, blacksmithing, weaving or textile design, is greatly admired.

African art had as profound an effect on modern Western art as Japanese prints had on Impressionism. Picasso, Modigliani, Derain, and countless others drew inspiration African sculpture, and nearly a century later, the jumpy background patterns of Keith Haring bear some relation to African prints.

Color symbolizes different things in different regions; these meanings may change from village to village, and even between families in the same village. Red is worn only by chiefs in Nigeria, but by everyone for mourning in Ghana, and is used for burial cloths in Madagascar.

Regions and Countries of Africa

Algeria

Mauritania
Green, which is a symbol of fertility, can be found in most of this region's flags. The crescent-and-star motif also appears more than once: on the Mauritania and Algerian flags.

Tanzania

Somalia
The design and colors of East Africa's flags can range from Somalia's understated white star centered on a blue field to Tanzania's blue and green fields divided by a broad strip of black bordered by yellow.

Angola

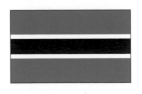

Botswana
Angola's flag is half red and half black with a yellow variation on the crescent-and-star motif. Botswana's banner is simply pale blue bisected by a black band.

West Africa: Algeria, Mauritania, Tanzania, Somalia, Angola, Botswana
Bold colors and patterns from tribal textiles of west Africa are rich with symbolism.

The societies with the biggest impact on the West African region are the Asante, Senufo, and Yoruba. Each of these has its own aesthetic traditions; fortunately there are few if any outright contradictions in color meanings between them. The Asante are renowned for their Kente cloth, a hand-woven fabric once reserved for royalty, but long in common use. Patterns and colors change according to local customs but there are a few general guidelines: dark colors are often (but not exclusively) associated with death, light colors with happy, festive occasions. The checkerboard and intertwining triangular patterns typical of the textiles of the Bwa and Mossi of Burkina Faso symbolize, through the contrasting of light and dark, the contrasts of nature; night and day, man and woman, good and evil.

East Africa
East Africa pales in its artwork and color palette.

The vast open grasslands of East Africa stretch across the countries of Kenya, Uganda, Ethiopia, Mozambique, the Sudan, Chad, Somalia, Congo (Zaire), and the Central African Republic. Pale wood carvings are more common and more popular in East Africa. There is less historical artwork and fewer traditional crafts from this region than elsewhere in Africa, perhaps because it has long been inhabited by nomads who were restricted to artwork that could be made quickly and was easily transported.

South Africa
In South Africa, colonial influences and vibrant native patterns mix to create a diverse spectrum.

What is now Capetown in the Republic of South Africa, was the halfway stop for ships making the long voyage between England and Australia, and from the 18th century was in regular contact with Europe. The colonizers of South Africa brought with them the color significance of their ancestral countries (Holland, France, and Britain), as did emigrants from India, Malaysia and elsewhere.

The exuberant zigzagging geometric and linear patterns painted on the exteriors of houses are characteristic of the Ndebele of South Africa. They have become emblematic of the region and stand in stark contrast to the uniformly white "Cape Dutch" style house favored by residents of European ancestry. The designs are not symbolic in and of themselves; instead, they reflect the creative whim of the painter, usually the woman of the house, who probably also makes fabric patterns of a similar design. With each repainting of the house, the design and palette may change. These repetitive and rhythmic patterns are typically bold colors; deep blues and reds are the most popular colors for backgrounds, with designs outlined in black or white. Elaborate beadwork is also a Ndebele craft; it can be so complex and delicate that it has to be taken apart to be taken off, and, therefore, may be worn for years. Stacks of copper bracelets, anklets and necklaces might also be worn for a lifetime.

In traditional ceremonial use, red means death and bloodshed. Red is worn only by chiefs in Nigeria but by everyone for mourning in Ghana, and is used for burial cloths in Madagascar. The nomadic Masai people of eastern Africa regions favor red fabrics, especially plaids and stripes. Because most adults of the Xhosa societies of South Africa wear red clothing, they are called the 'Red People.' Differing shades of red identify subgroup and village affiliations.

Green stands for fertility.

White is victory or purity and is worn by girls for puberty rites.

The Asante of West Africa adorn their chiefs and those of high rank in yellow.

THE COLORFUL LANGUAGE OF ZULU BEADWORK

Several southern African societies have a tradition of decorative beadwork; Zulu beadwork was also a form of communication, the colors and patterns noting an important event or conveying messages between lovers. The language of beadwork is mostly forgotten, but some of the color codes are still known. Red means passion or anger; black is darkness, trouble, or night. Blue has different meanings according to its shade. Dark blue is for elopement; medium blue means yearning; and pale blue, along with white, indicates pure love. Green stands for peace and joy. Brown means despondency or disgust. Zulu men and women routinely wear bead anklets, and today few artisans create beadwork for anything more than decorative purposes. Still, if one wishes to create a design that will resemble traditional Zulu beadwork, it is wise to verify through someone knowledgeable on the topic that your design does not have an unintended message or subtext.

Black implies age, maturity, and spirituality.

Gold signifies continuous life and is worn by the Asante queen mother.

The muted earth tones of the grassy savanna typify the East African palette. Its bright sunlight, dry climate, and dried grasses lead to the rust brown, yellows, oranges, and ochre that typify the palette of traditional fabrics. The Ewe silks of the Senufo (the Ivory Coast) are generally black, brown, or rust colored, and typically feature a patchwork quilt like grid-based design of a repeated pattern and variations.

In East Africa, blue beads are believed to enhance fertility. The danga, a turquoise necklace worn in South Africa to identify Xhosa to their ancestors, also identifies them to everyone else. Spiritual healers of the Xhosa wear white. Tanzania is known for tanzanite, a blue-violet gemstone that has recently become popular.

The Asoke cloth made by the Yoruba of Nigeria has metallic threads interwoven with cotton and rayon. This gives the cloth extra strength and durability and adds to its pattern. Indigo is the standard background color for the Yoruba's Adire cloth. Other colors are imposed on top of that through tie-dyeing or batik or painting. Because creating indigo dye is such a long and complex process, the color implies that much time, effort, and attention were invested in the making of the item on which it appears.

The Zebra's stripes on Starbucks Kenya Decaf logo stamp are used to represent duality bold favor in a decaffeinated coffee. "We made the graphics flat and bold, yet used colors that added a rich liveliness that we felt represented Africa. The typestyle was created to look like it was made from wood or something organic to blend well with the illustration," said Bonnie Dain, Starbucks designer. The coffee is not yet marketed in Africa, but is available in numerous other countries including the U.S., Canada, London, Saudi Arabia, China, Japan, and the Philippines.

PROJECT   STARBUCKS COFFEE COMPANY
                   KENYA DECAF COFFEE LOGO
DESIGN FIRM   STARBUCKS DESIGN GROUP
ART DIRECTOR   WRIGHT MASSEY
DESIGNER   BONNIE DAIN
CLIENT   STARBUCKS COFFEE COMPANY

Designers created the human figure on Starbucks' Kenya coffee logo to represent a Swahili dancer, an image they felt accurately reflected the coffee's rich flavor. The warm earth-tone color palette is also indicative of the region. "We wanted the Kenya stamp to reflect Kenya's rich culture and yet still take on a look that is unique to Starbucks," said Bonnie Dain, designer. The coffee is currently sold in the U.S., Canada, London, Saudi Arabia, China, Japan, and the Philippines, but is not yet available in Africa.

PROJECT	STARBUCKS COFFEE COMPANY KENYA COFFEE LOGO
DESIGN FIRM	STARBUCKS DESIGN GROUP
ART DIRECTOR	MICHAEL CORY
DESIGNER	BONNIE DAIN
ILLUSTRATOR	DAVID LEMLEY
CLIENT	STARBUCKS COFFEE COMPANY

The Asian Pacific Rim

Historically and culturally, China dominates Southeast Asia. Although each country in the region has its own unique customs, most can be traced back to Chinese origins. Chinese traditions regarding the significance and meanings of colors date to the Bronze Age, and over the centuries developed into a complex and formal color-symbol system. The good news for designers is that there are few taboos, although every color has accumulated thousands of years' worth of association and nuance. Even within the formal system of their symbolic meanings, colors embody multiple, even contradictory, characteristics, symbolizing both sides of the same coin: as the color of fire, red stands for both fire's creative and destructive aspects. Red is also the color associated with fertility, and, as is true universally, with shed blood. On another level altogether—the visual language of international commerce—red is also understood as the color of Coca-Cola cans and Marlborough cigarette packs, and the shades of red used on them in Kuala Lumpur are no different than in Cairo or Kalamazoo.

These color meanings also tie into the ancient practice of Feng Shui. The words translate literally as wind and water, and mean living in harmony with the environment. While it is neither a religion nor a philosophy, Feng Shui uses aspects of both in a blend of metaphysics, folklore, and earthy practicality. It is most commonly practiced regarding the design and placement of buildings; but it is routinely applied to everything from choosing the layout of an entire town to the arrangement of a desk and a chair within a room, and even the placement of wind chimes in a garden. The Chinese color symbols, as they relate to the five elements and points of the compass, apply in Feng Shui: a jewelry store's showroom might be painted white to evoke metal, which can indicate material success; white also stands for west and autumn, and might be used to connote these meanings as well. A shop selling wooden items might be painted green. These associative meanings can be important in product and package design.

In Asia, harmony and balance are overriding concerns in daily life. Contrasting colors are deliberately placed side by side as a display of balance between opposing elements, whether purely for decorative purposes or as a display of Buddhist philosophy. This might be done in equal portions, as in the Yin-Yang symbol (often depicted as black and white or red and yellow, or as a multiplicity of colors that when seen together create a vibrant, mosaiclike visual buzz). This sort of effect is best seen in the elaborate Buddhist temples of Thailand.

China, Hong Kong, and Taiwan

China
The flag of The People's Republic of China was patterned after the flag of the Soviet Union. Its red field symbolizes revolution and communism, and its five gold stars represent the five regions of China united in socialist goals.

Hong Kong
When it was still under British rule, Hong Kong's flag was a version of the Union Jack. Now, it consists of a red field with a white stylized flower in the center.

Taiwan
A stylized white sunburst pattern sits on a field of blue, designating Taiwan's flag.

Red is the primary color influence in Chinese culture, imbued with numerous connotations.

Bordered by fourteen other countries, China is the most populous nation on earth. Ruled by a succession of imperial dynasties from about 2200 BCE, in 1911 it became a republic. In 1949, Communist revolutionaries took over the government, established The People's Republic of China, and remain in power. Communist rule has diluted many folk traditions, but has not completely eradicated them.

In Hong Kong, Chinese color symbolism is rarely allowed to conflict with its bustling commercial center.

Long-time residents warn newcomers not to be fooled by the Western look of Hong Kong. Called the Manhattan of the Orient—and looking vaguely like San Francisco—Hong Kong has remained very Chinese through its century of British stewardship. However the British and multinational presence has had its effect in this capital of commerce. Hong Kong is an international island with a large community of non-Asians, and business is conducted with nearly every nation on earth. There is a vast assimilation of Western items; British, American, and Japanese products are considered of higher quality, and more fashionable, than the home-grown variety. English is widely used, and many signs, brand names, and company logos are as often displayed in their original language as they are translated into Chinese. The 1991 Hong Kong phone directory listed more advertising agencies than there are in New York City. But amid the steel and glass towers and choking traffic, traditional beliefs are more than merely quaint folklore; among them thinking as a group—a collective—as well as striving for harmony and balance in all aspects of life. Traditional Chinese color symbolism is understood and followed, but in this bustling commercial center it is rarely allowed to conflict with the needs of the marketplace. Feng Shui is practiced enthusiastically, as are astrology and numerology. Nearly three-quarters of the population adheres to Buddhist or Taoist principles.

In Taiwan, color use and theory follows the traditional Chinese model. One caution: due to overridingly anti-Communist sentiments in Taiwan, avoid anything that looks like the mainland's flag or any sort of socialist banner or signage.

The Taiwanese believe themselves to be the true heirs of traditional Chinese culture. When Communists took over Mainland China in 1949, the ousted republicans relocated eighty miles off the mainland, establishing themselves as the Republic of China on the provincial island of Formosa (now Taiwan). Traditional Chinese ways were re-established with a vengeance on Taiwan, and resentment toward the Communist government runs high. This island is a repository of Chinese traditions dotted with lavish temple complexes that bring together varied and disparate elements—divinities, icons, symbols—that would otherwise never reside in such close proximity; a living museum of Chinese culture.

Second and third-generation Taiwanese feel less of a link to the mainland, and the question of a move toward reunion, or to further their identity as a sovereign nation, is a matter of hot political debate. American influence has been strong from Taiwan's beginnings; many Taiwanese study in the U.S. and work for American companies. The island is a leading producer of athletic shoes, bicycles, PCs, televisions, and watches. Products and media from the U.S. are familiar, as are most brand names with a global reach. An entire generation of Taiwanese has grown up with McDonald's and American television; it is said that most Taiwanese under the age of thirty prefer hamburgers to egg rolls.

Red is inescapably associated with Communist China, and is linked with the southern region of the country, where the revolution began. That connection, in part, led to Communist China being referred to as "Red China." Chairman Mao's Little Red Book was a driving force during the Cultural Revolution of the 1960s. Although the most common iconography of the government is building-size portraits of its leaders, the motif of the flag of The People's Republic is echoed in other government identity; a huge red banner is almost certainly an official pronouncement.

Along with being the color symbol for fire, red means summer, the south, good luck, joy, good fortune, and fertility. It is the traditional color for a wedding dress (weddings are "red" ceremonies, one of the biggest occurrences in life). Red paper envelopes containing money are traditional Lunar New Years' gifts to children, and many companies give their employees annual bonuses in red envelopes at this time of year as well. Packages wrapped in red are given on happy occasions. A ruby is worn to promote long life. A notable exception to red's generally positive associations is that obituaries are traditionally written in red ink. Throughout Southeast Asia (and including Japan), a name written in red implies the end or severing of a relationship, if not the death of the one named. Red is also associated with southern China. Yellow or gold lettering on a red background is seen everywhere on signs, labels, and packaging.

Perhaps because the soil of northern China has a yellowish tone, yellow became the color symbol for earth. For several centuries, yellow was emblematic of and reserved for use exclusively by the Imperial family and still carries the echo of power and royalty. Yellow often symbolizes the masculine Yang (by contrast Yin would be red, and feminine) and the warmth and power of the sun. In the rest of Asia, yellow carries less political baggage, and is a color of joy, happiness, high spirits, and sunshine.

Blue signifies the sky and water, has positive associations, and is frequently used in decoration. Water is considered a feminine aspect of nature, and shades of blue are described in the Chinese language as shallow or deep rather than light or dark. There are no significant spiritual or mystical connotations for blue in Chinese traditions. Manual laborers have traditionally worn pale blue clothing (faded denim), although blue jeans are common for casual dress, regardless of wearer's job or social status.

The elements of nature, points of the compass, regions of the country, and the seasons all have corresponding colors in traditional Chinese color symbolism. The five elements and their colors are: earth (yellow); metal (white); water (black); wood (blue/green); and fire (red). Each color symbolically embodies physical and spiritual aspects of the element it represents. How and when these colors were used was often determined by the hierarchy of each element's attributes – fire overcomes wood, water overcomes fire, and so on; a life-size game of rock, paper, scissors. A white banner, symbolizing metal, might be the rallying color of an army attacking a feudal lord whose blue/green banners indicate wood. In Chinese mythology, the four kings of heaven that guard the compass points have different colored faces: north has a black face; south, red; east, green; west, white.

Along with being the color symbol for wood, green is also closely tied to jade, recalling its value and desirability. Green also represents the positive connotations of plants, crops, and spring. Green is the color of birth and youth—a wing of the Forbidden City that housed young princes was topped with green roof tiles. It is still considered a youthful color, especially in clothing, and implies exuberance and enthusiasm. The pear is a symbol of prosperity, perhaps owing to its pale, yellow/green color; however, note that the Chinese word for pear sounds much like the word for separate and has negative implications.

The color of love and happiness, orange has generally positive meanings. Buddhist monks wear saffron colored robes; once worn only by condemned criminals in India, the Buddha chose robes of this color to display his humility and rejection of worldly things. Orange draws significance from its blending of yellow and red, the colors of the Yin-Yang symbol, and although the color symbol for fire is red, when fire is seen in art it is rendered as orange/yellow. The orange is a symbol of happiness, plenitude, and good health, while peaches represent immortality.

Gold is prized not only for its preciousness, but for the radiance that objects plated with it take on. Gold of a deeper, darker hue is favored throughout Asia. Gold connotes prestige, wealth, and status, and its lavish display is not considered as ostentatious as it might be in the West; it is used on decorative objects, as an accent color, or as lettering, often on business cards. Gold lettering on a red background is the ultimate in prosperity.

Black is the color symbol for water, and therefore, carries all of the meaning and nuance that blue does for water in other cultures - depth, truth, life, stability. Black has little if any religious significance, but it does represent darkness and the unknown, and therefore mystery and even danger. It is the color of winter, and is associated with the northern regions of China (as red is to the South). Black is a common color for clothing because of its practicality. In Sumatra, clothing is made of from undyed cotton and worn until it becomes soiled, then dyed black. Black is also routinely used in lacquers and has a strong utilitarian tradition.

The color symbol for metal, white is also the color of death and mourning. Funerals, the second of the two most important passages in life, are "white" ceremonies (weddings, the previously mentioned "red" ceremonies, are the first). After cremation, the ashes of the deceased are placed in a white urn, and the family wears white linen for several weeks after the funeral. White clothing (an entire outfit, not merely a white shirt), packages, and flowers have strong funerary implications. White lettering on a dark background of any color, however, has no negative connotations, and neither does a white background containing text, or images surrounded by white space. An overabundance of white space around a small or isolated image or lettering, however, might hint at funerary meanings. White is also considered to be pure and neutral. In Hong Kong, white stands for west and autumn and might be used to connote these things.

IT'S VERY WELL MADE IN TAIWAN

■ Red was the logical choice for this logo used on Taiwan-made products that have been certified to meet the stringent standards of the national trade board. The tags come in different colors, but red is used exclusively in Asia.

PROJECT   TAIWAN-MADE LABEL/TAG

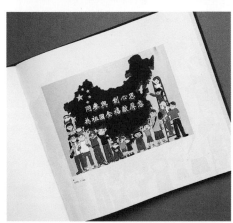

When Hong Kong dissolved its ties with Britain, it adopted China as its mother country. As an expression of good wishes to China on its 50th anniversary, children in Hong Kong created the drawings compiled in this book to celebrate. Not surprisingly, the color red dominates the book and "is the undisputed lucky color used in all kinds of celebrations," said Nick Tsui, art director. The cover also includes gold foil stamping, symbolizing prosperity and goodness. Multiple colors are used in the title to suggest youthfulness in keeping with the contents of the book. The cover drawing features a giant peach, selected because it is considered a good omen and signifies longevity in the Chinese culture. According to Tsui, peach-shaped buns are served at birthday banquets and the god of longevity is never depicted without a peach in his hand. Interestingly, many of the children's drawings included in the book rely heavily on red as dominant color scheme, showing just how powerful a color it is in the country.

Of special note, designers took special care to avoid setting blue characters on a white background as this combination is used on funeral lanterns and is taboo for all other occasions.

PROJECT	*TO MOTHER COUNTRY ON HER 50TH ANNIVERSARY*
DESIGN FIRM	CLIC LIMITED
ART DIRECTOR	NICK TSUI
DESIGNER	AMMESA CHAN
PRINTER	D & B PRODUCTIONS
CLIENT	HONG KONG SARDESIGN FIRM

The Phoenix Channel, a TV station on mainland China, uses a logo derived from the Yin-Yang symbol. The gold tone implies opulence and prestige, while the background color changes during this on-air promo from a jade green to the warm sunset tone seen here.

For the Asian Art Museum of San Francisco, Primo Angeli faced the challenge of creating an image representative of a vast geocultural diversity without compromising or slighting any aspect of it; it also had to be accessible and visually compelling for American viewers. Red, with its positive cross-cultural meanings, was the only real option.

PROJECT   ASIAN ART MUSEUM OF
               SAN FRANCISCO IDENTITY
DESIGNER   PRIMO ANGELI
CLIENT   ASIAN ART MUSEUM OF SAN FRANCISCO

In the lingering final frame of a lively animation and live action promo for Star TV, China, the Los Angeles-based broadcast graphics designers of 3 Ring Circus used a deep orange tone in the background to provide a warm glow, as well as a host of positive traditional meanings and associations; the logo's shimmering, radiant gold signals prestige, while the blue behind the gold provides contrast and balance. This color scheme was so successfully pan-Asian that for the version shown in India, the only changes necessary were the language and the replacement of this woman's face with that of an Indian woman.

PROJECT   STAR TV ANIMATION GRAPHICS
DESIGN FIRM   3 RING CIRCUS
CLIENT   STAR TV

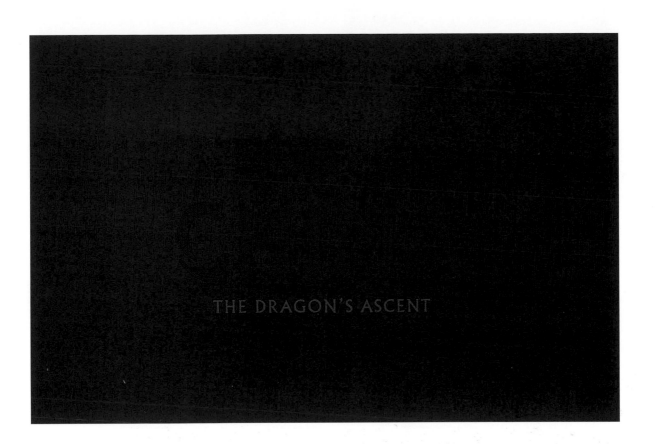

THE DRAGON'S ASCENT

154 · 155

■■ Designers at London-based Lewis Moberly created this logo for a ten-part television series on China and its contribution to the modern world. They gave the word China graphic dominance because it is strong, simple, and striking. They set it in a typeface to represent dragon's claws and colored it red—the positive color choice throughout China.

PROJECT	*CHINA: THE DRAGON'S ASCENT* LOGO
DESIGN FIRM	LEWIS MOBERLY
ART DIRECTOR	MARY LEWIS
DESIGNER	PAUL CHILIA LA CORTE
CLIENT	TOTEM PRODUCTIONS

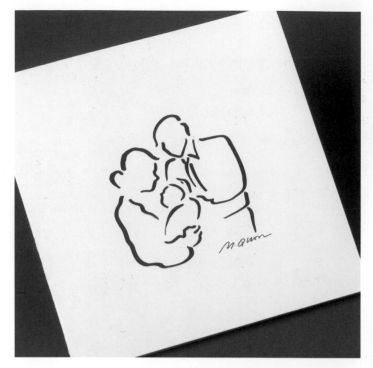

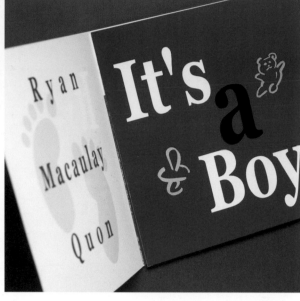

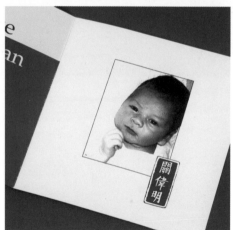

When New York designer Mike Quon's son was born, he created a birth announcement that paid tribute to his Chinese heritage. While many Western cultures commemorate births with pink for girls and blue for boys, red is the color of choice for births in China because it signifies good luck, happiness, and celebration. "Red was an easy choice because Ryan is half Chinese," said Mike Quon, pointing out that when money is given as a gift in China, it comes in a red envelope.

PROJECT   QUON BIRTH ANNOUNCEMENT
DESIGN FIRM   DESIGNATION INC.
ART DIRECTOR/
DESIGNER/
ILLUSTRATOR   MIKE QUON
CLIENT   QUON FAMILY

156 · 157

Mike Quon designed this notepaper for his firm's use employing a floral design steeped in Chinese color symbolism. Evocative of springtime, the design incorporates green, signifying the earth, eternal spirit, life, and growth and a blue-purple that when combined with green represents new beginnings and springtime.

PROJECT	NOTEPAPER
DESIGN FIRM	DESIGNATION INC.
ART DIRECTOR/	
DESIGNER/	
ILLUSTRATOR	MIKE QUON
CLIENT	DESIGNATION INC.

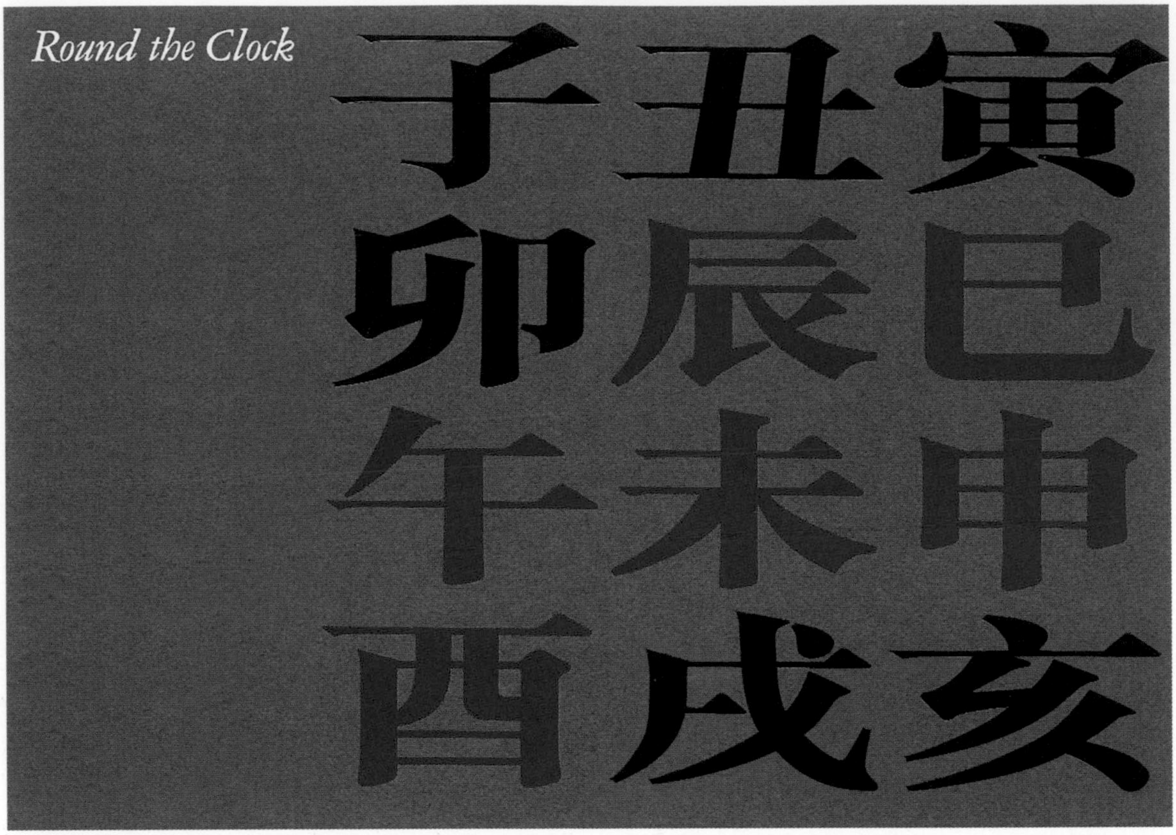

Round the Clock

子 丑 寅
卯 辰 巳
午 未 申
酉 戌 亥

■■ For a Hong Kong commercial real estate company that works round-the-clock, designer Henry Steiner used the twelve characters of the Chinese zodiac, which mark two-hour periods daily. The characters were colored red for daylight and black for nighttime.

PROJECT   REAL ESTATE "ROUND THE CLOCK" PROMOTION
DESIGNER   HENRY STEINER

Kan & Lau Design Consultants use the primary colors of red and yellow for the firm's 1998 Year of the Tiger lunar New Year card. By using these two colors together, designers created an eye-catching greeting card and conveyed their wishes for joy, happiness, and prosperity in the coming year.

PROJECT	LUNAR NEW YEAR CARD 1998- YEAR OF THE TIGER
DESIGN FIRM	KAN & LAU DESIGN CONSULTANTS
ART DIRECTORS	KAN TAI-KEUNG, FREEMAN LAU SIU HONG, EDDY YU CHI KONG
DESIGNER	VERONICA CHEUNG LAI SHEUNG
PHOTOGRAPHER	C.K. WONG
PRINTER	HONG KONG PRIME PRINTING CO. LTD.
CLIENT	KAN & LAU DESIGN CONSULTANTS

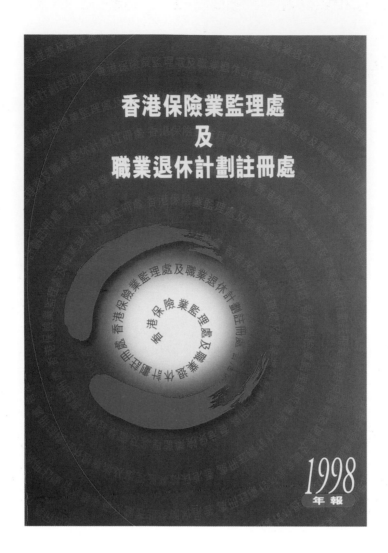

香港保險業監理處
及
職業退休計劃註冊處

香港保險業監理處及職業退休計劃註冊處
香港保險業監理處及
港保險業監理處及
險業監理處
香港保險業監理處及職業退休計劃註冊處

1998
年報

■ ■ A deep green sets the stage the Hong Kong Office of the Commissioner of Insurance Annual Report. It is the canvas onto which several other items of a symbolic nature are placed. The glowing sphere places the Office of the Commissioner of Insurance at the center of the industry. The spiraling name symbolizes the office's extensive influence. The abstract "embracing arms" stand for agency priority to protect the public interest, while the arc on the left symbolizes the self-disciplinary measures adopted by the insurance industry.

PROJECT	OFFICE OF THE COMMISSION OF INSURANCE ANNUAL REPORT
DESIGN FIRM	CLIC LIMITED
ART DIRECTOR	NICK TSUI
DESIGNER	AMMESA CHAN
CLIENT	OFFICE OF THE COMMISSIONER OF INSURANCE
PRINTER	HONG KONG GOVERNMENT PRINTER

Singapore and Malaysia

The red of the hibiscus unified the many diverse cultures of the region.

Singapore
Singapore's flag is a horizontal bar of red-orange above an equal-sized bar of white. In the upper band are a white crescent, representing Islam, and five stars in a circle that stand for Singapore's Five Ideals democracy, peace, progress, justice and equality.

Malaysia
The Malaysian flag resembles the flag of the United States. Fourteen horizontal stripes represent the equal status of the thirteen Malay states and their federal government. The canton of dark blue displays the unity of the Malaysian people, the crescent represents Islam, and the fourteen-point starburst the unity of the states and government. The yellow of the crescent and star is the royal color.

Singapore is a fascinating nation. With no natural resources, its entire population is descended from immigrants; it owes its existence to other countries' need for a gateway to Asia. Physically part of Malaysia, and linked by common threads of culture and history, Singapore has its own identity; to work successfully there requires a better-than-passing knowledge of every culture in the region.

Singapore is a mix of cultures: the predominant Chinese (known as Straits Chinese), Indian, and Malaysian cultures, with a thick overlay of British colonialism. These diverse cultures have not blended to create a hybrid. The traditions of each group are known to the others. Most major religious holidays and celebrations that are held in public have taken on a secular, street-fair element; everyone participates in—or at least watches—the festivities. Malaysia has a similar mix of peoples but in different proportions; primarily, there are far fewer ethnic Chinese, and more Moslems.

The red hibiscus is the Malaysian national flower; a revered national symbol, it is still used in herbal medicine as a cure for everything from skin ailments and fevers to headaches. During the religious festivals that honor the Monkey God, mediums channel his words, writing them in their own blood on bits of paper that become amulets to devotees.

Yellow has long been the color of Malaysian royalty, and is still associated with those in authority. Throughout Malaysia, taxicabs have yellow roofs (although the rest of the car may be another color). Public phones that require a phone card to make a call are yellow.

In Singapore and Malaysia, green designates one's affiliation with Islam. A twig or branch with leaves or greenery still on it is placed at the rear of a car parked at the roadside to signal that it is disabled and that help is needed.

Coin-operated public phones in Malaysia are orange-colored.

Black clothing is worn to funerals in the Western manner, even by Malay Chinese who otherwise follow the traditional Chinese color traditions.

White chrysanthemums are used in important ceremonial pilgrimages.

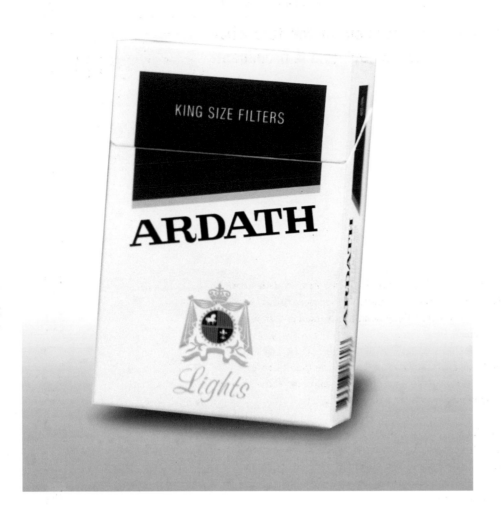

■□ Ardath cigarettes are marketed to and sold in Singapore, but the product's packaging design shares its heritage with the Indonesian color scheme. Red and white are the two primary colors in the flags of both Singapore and Indonesia, the latter where red represents the human factor and the white represents spiritual influences. In this case, red was chosen for its power, vigor, and psychological link to excitement. "Its stimulating power can be effective on products such as coffee, cola, cigarettes, or energy-drinks," said Jonathan Bonsey. "Another association to red comes from the word *Abangan*. This Indonesian term comes from the Javanese word *abang* (red) and describes a big part of the rural Muslin communities whose culture strongly reflects the influence of Buddhism and Hinduism, which originated in India and preceded the Islam era."

PROJECT   ARDATH CIGARETTE BRAND IDENTITY
DESIGN FIRM   BONSEY DESIGN PARTNERSHIP
ART DIRECTOR   JONATHAN BONSEY
DESIGNER/
ILLUSTRATOR   MARK CHUNG
CLIENT   BRITISH AMERICAN TOBACCO MARKETING

Thailand

Color use in Thailand is purely for decorative purposes—and gold is prominent.

Thailand's current flag was adopted in 1917 when a blue stripe was added to the horizontal white bar, bordered top and bottom by red stripes, that was its predecessor.

Color use in Thailand is distinguished from that in the rest of Southeast Asia by its unabashed use for purely decorative purposes. Even a small Buddhist temple will feature intricate carvings and a statue of Buddha encrusted with gold; ordinary fishing boats are painted in such elaborate designs as to rival a Taiwanese dragon boat.

Thailand has a profusion of flowers, and they are commonly used for decoration; there are 1,000 species of orchids in Thailand, and flowers are visible everywhere. Marigolds and carnations are flowers that are used for funerals, and therefore associated with death.

Many travelers and traders have passed along the Mekong River that flows from Tibet to southern tip of the Vietnamese seacoast, and Thailand has absorbed their influence. In the phrase of a guidebook, this is "a land of contrasts." While Bangkok is a thoroughly modern, Westernized city, complete with traffic jams and neon-lit streets, the countryside is rural and remote. Thailand as a whole is still more agricultural than industrial.

The use of gold is the most striking aspect of the Thai aesthetic. It is used everywhere and on virtually everything, from the traditional neck rings worn by Karen tribeswomen to the tall spires of Buddhist temples. Inside many temples, colored tiles are set into a lacy grillwork of gold to create a glowing multicolored effect. Pattern is as important a decorative element as color. This is obvious in architecture that includes the prang, corncob textured stone or concrete reliquary-towers in temples, and the elaborately beaded and brocaded ceremonial costumes and traditional folk dress of the country.

Nearly 95 percent of the Thai population is Buddhist; the saffron colored robes of Buddhist monks are a common sight. Ordination as a monk isn't necessarily a lifetime commitment; many Thai men will spend anywhere from a few days to several years as monks.

Yellow sashes are often placed around Buddha statues to indicate the state of nirvana.

■■ Attendees of Creasia, a creative conference in Bangkok, received this bright red notebook, created in red because of its Chinese association with good fortune and wealth. The logo for the conference was an eye, so designers faxed all participants and requested information on their eye color. They used their feedback to have glass eyeballs manufactured to match everyone's eye color and placed them in die-cut holes in the notebook.

PROJECT	CREASIA CONFERENCE NOTEBOOK
DESIGN FIRM	THE DESIGN GROUP
ART DIRECTOR	STEFAN SAGMEISTER
DESIGNERS	STEFAN SAGMEISTER, PETER RAE, MIKE CHAN, ANDREW POGSON
COPYWRITER	STEFAN SAGMEISTER
PRINTER	ASIA PACIFIC
CLIENT	LEO BURNETT ASIA

South Korea

Once deeply ingrained, color meanings have been jettisoned in modern South Korea.

The South Korean flag features a red and blue yin-yang symbol, ringed by four images from the I-Ching which sit in the center of a white field that stands for purity. An update of the traditional royal flag of Korea, this version was adopted by South Korea after World War II.

Traditional and historical color meanings have little or no place in the daily lives of most Koreans. In its drive to become a completely modern country, South Korea jettisoned many of its traditional ways; what is remarkable is that the color coding of Korean life up through the late 19th century was more elaborate and strictly enforced than anything a Chinese emperor could have dreamed up. Confucianism was the official philosophy of the Yi dynasty (1832-1910), and its doctrine of strict adherence to hierarchical structure was firmly institutionalized. The clothing of courtiers and palace workers was color-coded to signal their function and rank. Among commoners, the color of a person's clothing—hats especially—could indicate their social standing, marital status, or profession. The American presence in South Korea since 1945 has had a great effect on this society; Koreans learned mass communication from the Americans, and many American products are known there. Feelings toward Japan and the Peoples' Republic of China are ambivalent.

Good luck in Korea, as elsewhere in Asia, comes in red. The proper dress for attendants of the 19th century royal court was a cloak of red gauze over a blue robe. Red ribbons or red cuffs were worn as remembrance of the blood shed by heroes. The member of a wedding party who carried in the goose for the feast would do so wearing a ceremonial red hat hired for the event.

Along with its appeal as a color of joy and happiness, yellow in Korea was the traditional color of the straw hat worn by someone engaged to be married.

Dark blue is a color of mourning. Minor court officials of the Yi dynasty wore dark blue, usually adorned with embroidery of storks or tigers. In Korea as elsewhere, denim has gone from the standard clothing for manual laborers to everyday casual wear.

A popular accent color in dress, and the metal of choice for royal emblems, gold is characteristically used for plating statuary.

For Koreans, black has combined Asian and Western meanings. It is the color of darkness, mystery, and mourning; it also carries the associations of the Chinese color symbol for water. A black hat band with the emblem of a gold bird was worn only by Yin dynasty royalty, while a black horsehair hat was exclusively for scholars learned in Chinese classics.

Vertex, a fictional Korean automobile manufacturer, was dreamed up by Germany's Braue Design. For a self-promotion, the design firm created a logo and key chain for the carmaker, giving the fictitious entity many of the design characteristics we've come to associate with German performance cars. The upscale look comes from the silver logo and metallic colors incorporated into the collateral materials pictured with the key chain. Together, these colors signify upscale luxury—whether the country is Germany or Korea. "First, we came up with a name for the company that said 'sportive, high-tech, and aggressive,'" said Kai Braue, Braue Design. "A stylish, element symbol, accompanied by an advertising campaign aiming for the luxury-oriented young urban professionals were our solutions."

PROJECT	VERTEX MOTOR CORPORATION LOGO AND KEY CHAIN
DESIGN FIRM	BRAUE DESIGN
ART DIRECTOR/ DESIGNER	MARÇEL ROBBERS
CLIENT	BRAUE DESIGN

Indonesia

Brightly colored batik patterns are the most visible example of color usage in Indonesia.

The flag of Indonesia is simplicity itself, a horizontal bar of red set on top of an equal-sized bar of white.

Indonesia is an archipelago of more than 10,000 islands, the principal of these being Java, Bali, Borneo, western New Guinea, Kalimantan, and Sumatra. It is the fourth most-populous country on earth, and its larger cities—Jakarta, Kuala Lumpur—look like those of any other bustling Asian port city, complete with high-rise office towers, American fast food, Mercedes and BMWs honking at traffic lights, and billboards advertising Coca-Cola, Sony, and Kodak.

There is no formal system of color symbolism in Indonesia; its islands are too numerous and too scattered, and it has only been a unified country since 1949. Parts of Indonesia have been colonized and fought over by European and Asian powers for centuries, but trade is most responsible for shaping its cultural melange. The country's motto is "Unity in Diversity," an acknowledgment of the great variations in language and local customs that make a truly homogenous culture unthinkable.

Despite the absence of specific symbolism, color has played a pivotal role in the history of Indonesia. Islanders eagerly traded plentiful local spices for pigments and dyes brought on merchant ships, and the elaborate and colorful batik and textiles created from them in turn became valuable commodities that brought high prices from visiting traders. There are no set rules or meanings regarding design and color use in the making of fabrics, although a woven blanket or cloth is part of life-cycle rituals, presented at ceremonial rites of passage such as birth, marriage, and death.

Red ink indicates that you are angry at whomever you've written to. The red headbands worn by men of the Naulu tribe on the island of Seram signal their adherence to ancient tribal ways. A traditional Indonesian wedding dress is red with gold embroidery.

Indigo, easily available on Java, made blue one of the oldest known background colors for batik and woven fabrics. Among the Chinese Indonesians, blue is a color of sadness.

Gold is prized more for its decorative than monetary value (although expense and rarity are factors in its use). Yellowish colors that approach gold are often used with a bright red or deep blue background. The Garuda, a mythical golden bird, is the national symbol of Indonesia.

One of the earliest Indonesian dyes produced browns in a wide range of shades from a dark, earthy color to rust and almost orange. These were used for patterns and designs on backgrounds of vivid reds and deep blues.

Japan

Few societies reveal as much of their character through color use as Japan.

The red circle in a white background of the Japanese flag symbolizes a rising sun, and is also the Imperial mon. The imperial banner for 1,500 years, it became the national flag in 1870. The white background represents purity and honesty.

International economist Max Mohl has described Japan as being "Lotusland and robotland — two levels of existence that cannot easily be reconciled . . . Nor does anyone want to reconcile them." The country's aesthetic seems to have a split personality (Zen gardens vs. Mighty Morphin Power Rangers), and the balancing of disparate elements is an essential component in the culture. Few societies reveal as much of their character through their use and organization of color as the Japanese.

Japan, like Europe, developed a system of heraldry. These emblems or mons were circular, and often of an elaborate geometric or floral pattern. Mons were not always colored, but the red circle of the modern Japanese flag is the mon of the emperor, its red insignia symbolizing the imperial family's claim of descendancy from the goddess of the sun.

The headbands worn by Japanese workers are a show of purposefulness and concentration. Team members or company workers may wear headbands of the same color, or decorated with an appropriate emblem or logo. Student protesters have worn white helmets as a variation on this theme; it serves as a display of their sincerity as well as protection, and provides a striking contrast with the black helmets and uniforms of the police.

The ubiquitous national color, red is seen on the flag, public phones, in advertising, print materials, and television graphics. The kesa (ceremonial robes) of the second most senior Zen Buddhist abbot is red. Cherries symbolize self sacrifice; their red flesh symbolizes blood, and passion. Although not exclusively, red ink is used to signal the end of a relationship (a less extreme version of the Chinese use of red ink for obituaries). Red is a common lacquer color, implying strength and durability. Lobsters are symbols of long life and common gifts at New Year.

A popular accent color in clothing and gardening, yellow is the color worn by a Zen monastery's third most senior abbot. Yellow has virtually no negative connotations, and is usually associated with sunshine and flowers.

Blue comes in three strengths: deep, medium, and washed out. Work clothes are blue, and American blue jeans of all shades are popular. Traditional yukatas (bathrobes) are decorated with elaborate blue and white prints.

In muted and soft, nature-based tones, green is much loved but not much used in decoration or dress, except as an accent. More vibrant green, however, is used in modern signage. The next-to-lowest ranking abbot in a Zen monastery wears a green kesa.

This color represents love and happiness, and is closely associated with its eponymous fruit and like-colored flowers. Orange is also the color of Buddhist monks' robes, although they are seen less often here than in other countries with significant Buddhist populations.

For centuries deep violet was almost exclusively an imperial color, not—at least initially—for its symbolic value, but simply because the dyes were too costly for anyone but royalty. For similar reasons, only the highest-ranking abbot of a Zen monastery was entitled to wear purple ceremonial robes. Violet and purples of various shades are favored because of their rarity in nature and the pleasing contrast they create with more common colors; gardeners routinely place violet flowers next to buttercups or other yellow flowers.

Pink is a popular accent color in clothing, and the color of racy humor (as blue is in the U.S.). The pink-blossoming cherry tree is a national symbol. Pink means spring, femininity, and youth; though the peony, the Imperial flower, is linked to masculinity, riches, and good fortune. Pink is a traditional color for women's undergarments because of the belief that it promotes proper blood circulation and, therefore, good health.

The Japanese language has no single word that covers all shades of "brown." Instead, brown tones are described by comparison tea-colored, fox-colored, wood-colored, etc. Earth tones play a key part of the Shibui tradition, and the color of a material evokes its characteristics. Tree, for example, can signal strength and durability. The fourth level of monastic seniority wears a brown kesa.

Japanese Buddhas and other statuary are often made of bronze, in contrast to the gold Buddhas seen in Southeast Asia. The largest Buddha statue in the world, at Nara, Japan, is bronze. Bronze's earthy color and durability makes it pleasing to the Japanese aesthetic; its eventual green patina only enhances the effect. For this reason, other earthy metals, like copper and brass, are widely used for these reasons.

Not as widely used for decoration as elsewhere in Asia, gold is valued nonetheless. Lavish displays of gold are considered garish, and run counter to the Japanese tradition of modesty (at least in public); an old proverb tells that "Riches are but clouds and smoke." During the 18th century, it was a punishable offense to show off or brag about amassed wealth. Still, gold is an unambiguous symbol of wealth and prestige.

Silver, steel, and similarly colored metals are associated with tools and weaponry; the meaning is generally masculine, and recently high-tech, with implications of precision and strength. Samurai swords were finely crafted and valuable objects aside from their usefulness as weapons; a well-made sword was treasured and passed down through a family for generations.

THE SIGNIFICANCE OF JAPANESE PRINTS

The effect of Japanese prints on 19th century Western art is well known and clearly visible in the compositions of Edgar Degas, the flatness and brush strokes of James McNeill Whistler, the glittering gold-leaf patterns of Gustav Klimt, and the stylized mon-inspired signature of Henri Toulouse-Lautrec. What is less known is the effect of Western art on the Japanese. Hokusai is remembered in his homeland not as an artist who made an impression on the Impressionists, but for reintroducing bright color into Japanese printmaking (for which he was accused of vulgarity by contemporaries). Because he used the bright blue inks newly imported from Europe, he had to adjust the rest of his palette to balance their

The color of non-being, and non-existence (see Kabuki Influence), although not necessarily death is symbolized by black. It is also the color of night, the unknown, and mystery. Crows are messengers of Shinto gods. Someone in a foul or angry mood is said to have a black face. The lowliest abbot in a Zen monastery wears a black kesa. A common color for lacquers, a black object implies strength and durability. The second-most popular color for cars, black is the usual color for the housings and casings of cameras and electronics equipment. In the 1980s several Japanese companies manufactured cameras and television sets in bright colors, but they sold so poorly that they were discontinued.

Although white is a color of mourning and death in Japan, as elsewhere in Asia, it also has very positive aspects. It is the most popular color for cars in Japan, and the color of martial arts practice clothing. On the flag and in most symbolic uses, white stands for purity and honesty. White Western-style wedding dresses have become popular with Japanese brides; in addition to being fashionable, the white also serves as a display that the bride is now symbolically dead to her family. In Shinto mythology, a white fox is a divine messenger.

Shibui and Kabuki Color Influences

There are two distinct, yet culturally inseparable, approaches to color use. Both are intricate and varied, and create a pleasing look through a balance of color, texture, and proportion.

The first method is Shibui, which, although it means, literally, "non-color," looks to nature as a model for achieving aesthetic equilibrium; balance based on complementary or related tones. Shibui grew out of Zen painting, marked by the use of gradations of gray and black, and the emphasis of tone and hue over color. The Shibui palette is characterized by broken or grayed colors used in a way that avoids strong contrasts of hue, and emphasizes soft, muted tones off-white, beige, grays, browns, mauve, often with an accent of pink, blue, red, or green. In interior design, architecture, dress, and most aspects of personal life, Shibui is a way of organizing and coordinating colors (brightly colored kimonos are made for export only; most Japanese consider them really tacky). The Japanese Zen garden—intended as a microcosm of the universe—is a model of Shibui principles. The subdued palette promotes contemplation and leads to serenity, without the use of too many colors that would 'confuse the eye and bewilder the mind.' Color use is also much influenced by the local climate, and reflects Japan's constantly changing sky, frequent rain (whether a surface is glossy or matte—wet or dry—is almost as important a distinction as its color), and the resulting rich greens of plant life. The nature-revering spirit of the native Shinto religion also contributes to this overall aesthetic.

The other primary source of color use is the theatrical tradition of Kabuki. In Kabuki, the coordination of makeup and costume is a choreography of color that provides a striking visual tableau at every moment of the performance. It is as important an element as the sound or the acting. Costumes of stock characters follow certain conventions and coordinate with the colors of the other characters on-stage. Precise colors change with each production, and every city and region has its own color scheme. A character's importance is signaled by whether its costume's colors play against those of others, as well as the intensity of color and ornateness of design.

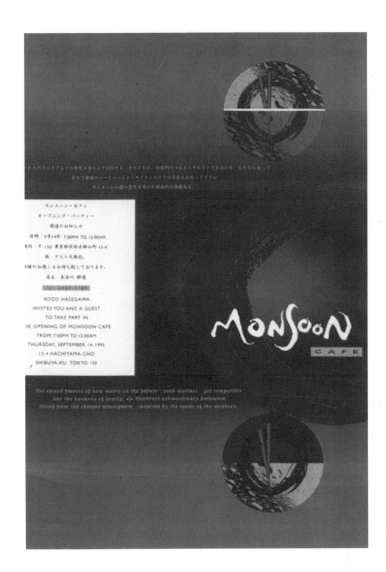

■ ■ ■ ■ For an invitation to the opening of a restaurant in Tokyo that serves pan-Asian cuisine, Vrontikis Design employed orange, red, and green, all of which have positive meanings throughout the region, then added a dash of purple, which is a popular accent color in Japan, on this subway poster. Together, the colors represent the vibrancy of Asian cultured unified by the Monsoon season.

Petrula Vrontikis points out that although the color palette appears Asian to Western countries, in the context of Tokyo subway stations, it stood out in stark contrast to other advertising. "We proposed more muted tones, but our client wanted bright, dynamic 'hot' colors," said Vrontikis.

"It was interesting to have an American designer interpret Asian culture," Vrontikis added. "My client wants to promote an international cosmopolitan look. We provide that perfectly, but it's not as premeditated as one might imagine. My work with this client in the Tokyo marketplace has a wonderful dynamic energy about it that seems universal."

PROJECT	MONSOON CAFÉ GRAND OPENING POSTER/INVITATION
DESIGN FIRM	VRONTIKIS DESIGN
ART DIRECTOR	PETRULA VRONTIKIS
DESIGNER	KIM SAGE

■ ■ The color theme for the signage and decor of Canal City, a shopping center in Japan, was chosen to represent elements of nature and the universe. The input of local designers helped Selbert Perkins Design create a program of color that truly resonates with the center's clientele. Yellow evokes the sun, blue stands for the effect of the moon on tides and the rhythms of life; the red, of course, means good fortune everywhere in Asia. The copper statue within the mall extends the universe theme.

PROJECT   **CANAL CITY SIGNAGE**
DESIGN FIRM   **SELBERT PERKINS DESIGN**
CLIENT   **CANAL CITY**

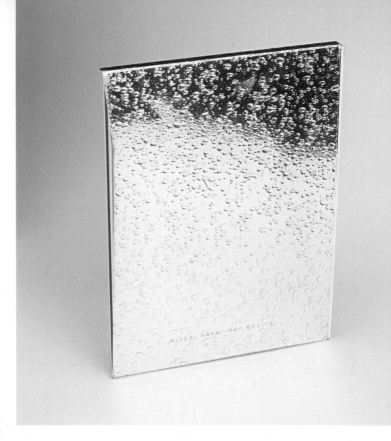

Revival is a collection of typographic design work that Hideki Nakajima has created since he began work as art director for Cut, a Japanese magazine. The book is comprised of typographical images—specifically, the names of celebrities that have been featured in the magazine—that Nakajima creates by photographing three-dimensional objects made of metal, wood, and acrylic materials. Although the book's primary purpose is to showcase Nakajima's original typography, it is also provides a tour of the color spectrum.

One gets their first impression of the book from its slipcase that is made from a metallic silver paper on which drops of water are printed by a special process—foreshadowing the natural materials to follow in the typographic images. The book cover and inside cover spread are embossed, but relatively devoid of color—the former in white and the latter in silver. These pages transition to the black title page. From there, the black gives way, little by little, to peaks of light—primarily, a metallic blue hue—until the next section of typographic images are shown in the blue of blueprints.

With Hugh Grant's page, the color palette gets lively, using gradations of single shades. After that, readers are treated to other color combinations and ultimately arrive at a section devoted to primary hues. The book takes readers through a display of steely gray and black pages, before transitioning to images reminiscent of sepia-toned vintage prints. From there, type treatments revert to mixed primary colors and eye-popping bold colors, before the pages gradually lose their color and return to black and then white once again.

The palette is not typically Japanese, but reflects a universal usage of color, not unlike the universal recognition factor of the celebrities featured.

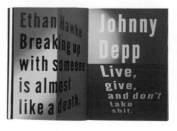

PROJECT   REVIVAL, A COLLECTION OF TYPOGRAPHIC
              DESIGN WORK
DESIGN FIRM   NAKJIMA DESIGN CO., LTD.
ART DIRECTOR/
DESIGNER   HIDEKI NAKAJIMA
PHOTOGRAPHER   VARIOUS
CLIENT   ROCKIN' ON INC.

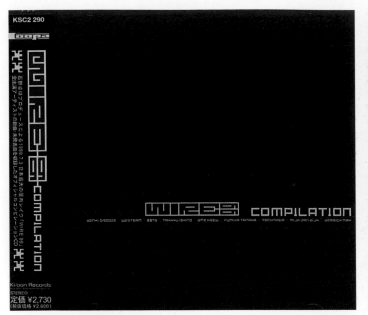

■■□■ Frame Graphics was responsible for the design of everything for WIRE '99, a large-scale music event held in Japan's Yokohama Arena, from the promotional posters to retail items including T-shirts, album and CD packaging, and lighters. Designers fashioned the logo for versatility—it had to work equally well on over-sized items as well as small pieces. They gave the event's name a bold typographic treatment against a color palette of red, white, blue, and black—colors inspired by the signage found in the arena.

PROJECT   WIRE '99 T-SHIRTS, ALBUM, AND CD
CLIENT   STONE BROKE INC.
DESIGN FIRM   FRAME GRAPHICS CO., LTD.
ART DIRECTOR   HIDEYUKI TANAKA
DESIGNERS   HIDEYUKI TANAKA, MANAMI TIJIMA

Café La Boheme, an exclusive restaurant in Tokyo, offers an eclectic menu that blends Italian and Japanese cuisine. To announce its grand opening, Vrontikis Design Office created a subway poster that graphically illustrates the blending of cuisines while reflecting the restaurant's interior décor. For the background pattern, Petrula Vrontikis used a photo of a Florentine ceiling pattern that was shot in the Ufizzi Gallery in Florence, Italy. She simplified the pattern and colored it red because the shade is thought to be the national color of Japan. The image of the woman is taken from a painting that the restaurant owner purchased in Paris and that now hangs in the restaurant. "The 'international eclectic' aspect of the piece was important to convey," explained Vrontikis. "This color scheme along with the symbols communicated well to the Japanese audience."

Project	Café La Boheme Subway Poster
Design Firm	Vrontikis Design Office
Art Director/	
Designer/	
Photographer	Petrula Vrontikis
Client	Global Dining, Inc.

India

Hindu symbolism and color meanings dominate Indian culture and society.

The Indian flag is made up of three equal horizontal bars orange at the top, white in the middle, and green along the bottom. In the center of the white stripe sits the image of a Buddhist wheel of life.

India is a kaleidoscope of vivid colors. Colors must to be bright—even gaudy—to hold up outdoors under the glare of the blazing sun. Calcutta is twenty-two degrees north of the equator, and the sunlight there is twice as intense as that of London. This fact accounts for the traditional use of brilliant color in theater, festivals, and any situation where it will be seen in sunlight. During Holi, the boisterous celebration of the end of winter, colored powders (any and all colors) are tossed onto everybody and everything. People tend to wear clothing they either don't mind getting colored or deliberately opt for white to provide a good blank canvas.

Indian brides wear a red wedding dress as a symbol of the birth of a new phase of their life, and for fertility; a red bindi and red powder along the part in a woman's hair signifies that she is married. Although, for women the bindi, (usually red) is to be worn on the forehead after worshipping. Many urban Indian women have taken to wearing the bindi as purely decorative, color coordinating it with their clothing; even non-Hindu women have taken up the fashion. Rubies are associated with royalty, dignity, zeal, and power. The Kshatriya (warrior) caste is signified by red. The guna Raja's color is red, associated with red meat and hot spices like onions and garlic. Red is also the color of Lakshami, the goddess of wealth and beauty. More prosaically, red is the packaging color for Lifebuoy bath soap, the country's largest selling brand.

Yellow represents the sun and its power; during various spring festivals people wear yellow clothing, eat yellow food, and sprinkle yellow powder (tumeric) over statues of the god appropriate to the occasion. Yellow is associated with the Vaisya or merchant caste. Taxis, and auto-taxis (which resemble three-wheeled, motorized rickshaws) are yellow and black in every major city in India. Nirma detergent powder, a popular national brand, comes in a yellow package.

Blue has nearly universally positive meanings in the Indian subcontinent. Krishna has blue skin, symbolizing the heavens, love, truth, and mercy, as well as the mysterious nature of truth. Hinduism said that truth is often hidden in mystery, so the darker the color, the deeper the mystery, and perhaps the greater the truth being concealed.

The color of plants and crops, green is a very positive color in this largely arid landscape. In the traditional music and dance form called Kathakali, the performers who are playing the parts of the "good guys" have their faces painted green.

Pink is a happy, hopeful color. Pink powder is tossed all around during the closing parades of celebrations of the birth of Ganesh.

Like Buddhist monks throughout Asia, Hindu monks' robes are saffron. Traditionally, a married woman's death shroud would be orange.

Negative to neutral connotations surround black in India. The Sudra—untouchable—caste has black as its attendant color. Laziness, anger, indolence, and a host of bad character traits are ascribed to the guna Tamas, whose color is black. Foods associated with Tamas include smoked or preserved meats, mushrooms, and alcohol.

White has predominantly positive associations in India. It is the color of all things Brahman; the god, the caste (the highest), and the "sacred cows." White is also associated with milk— the food of the gods—and virtually all dairy foods as well as nuts, seeds, fruits, vegetables, and grains. Hindu mythology has a milky ocean as the source of all creation. Through the guna Sattva, white stands for knowledge, light, and serenity. Hindu holy men cover themselves in ash to symbolize their renunciation of earthly things and their spiritual rebirth. On the less-than-upbeat side, the death shrouds of men and widows are white; the notion of reincarnation somewhat mitigates the negative symbolism of things surrounding death rites and ceremonies.

The British Influence

Two hundred years of occupation by the British left many imprints on Indian culture, but color was not one of them. The exception is in advertising and packaging, where mimicking the color, design, and even the names of well-known English items is commonplace. Actually, India left a bigger impression on Britain, giving the English a wide range of spices, and the color khaki (the Hindi word for "dust") which was adopted for military uniforms.

With eighty percent of the population as followers, the Hindu faith is the single biggest influence on Indian life, and the symbolism and color meaning derived from it dominate the culture. There are two sets of elements that are key to the color significance of Hinduism.

First are the gunas. The concepts of the cosmos and the world are the three gunas, each of which has a corresponding color. Basic Hindu principles relate color to various stages of being The first guna, Sattva, is white, and represents calmness, brightness, and the light of knowledge; next is Raja, red, for activity, passion, and energy; the third is Tamas, symbolized by black for its laziness, anger, and lack of purpose.

Secondly are the major divinities. Among Hunduism's 330 million divinities (roughly one for every three Indians), there are three prominent gods from whom spring dozens of subsidiary manifestations. They are Brahma (also called Ishwara or Mahashakti), the creator, is the top dog and whose perfect state is the goal of reincarnation and whose color is white; Vishnu (also called Rama or Krishna), the protector, among whose many incarnations the most popular and frequently pictured is the blue-skinned, flute-playing Krishna; Shiva (also called Nataraja, Parvati, or Kali), is the destroyer, fearsome and black skinned. Kali embodies both the end-of-life cycle of Hinduism, and the mysterious and terrible power of women.

By far the most popular Hindu divinity is the smiling, pink elephant-headed Ganesha. Beloved, friendly, and usually benevolent, Ganesha—and pink—is associated with optimism and hope for good fortune.

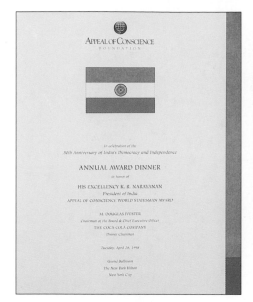

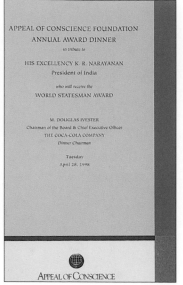

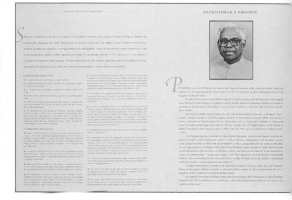

The Appeal of Conscience Foundation, an organization that promotes world peace, honored the President of India at its annual award dinner. Lieber Brewster Design, Inc., created the invitation, event brochure, and program using the colors (orange, white, and green) and a graphic representation of the Indian flag as the identifying theme, which also unified the three individual elements. "...[W]e carefully matched colors to an actual flag and employed an abstracted flag motif, adapting the design to the various formats," explains Anna Lieber. When working with designs for cultures that are not your own, designers must not only be sensitive to color usage, but other design elements as Lieber discovered. "Extremely exacting rules of protocol were addressed with respect to usage of President Narayanan's photograph."

PROJECT   **APPEAL OF CONSCIENCE FOUNDATION INVITATION, BROCHURE, AND EVENT PROGRAM**
DESIGN FIRM   **LIEBER BREWSTER DESIGN, INC.**
CREATIVE DIRECTOR/
DESIGNER   **ANNA LIEBER**
CLIENT   **APPEAL OF CONSCIENCE FOUNDATION**

Unilever's Rexona has nearly 80 percent brand awareness among more than one billion people in
Bangladesh, Pakistan, Sri Lanka, and India; consequently, designers at Bonsey Design Partnership found
it difficult, if not impossible, to create a new package
design for the product using colors with specific cultural or religious associations because of the enormity of
the market. However, in Pakistan and India, the green
and yellow Rexona package is as widely recognized as
Coca-Cola's red packaging throughout the world,
according to the design firm, so the creative team
strived to maintain this color recognition while integrating the country's four different product identities
into one single brand identity. The bright green symbolizes freshness, health, and cleanliness; the yellow
communicates care and softness. This is further
emphasizes by the golden drop of oil—symbolizing
purity and richness.

PROJECT	REXONA BRAND IDENTITY
DESIGN FIRM	BONSEY DESIGN PARTNERSHIP
ART DIRECTOR	JONATHAN BONSEY
DESIGNER/	
ILLUSTRATOR	MIA WATTEN
CLIENT	UNILEVER

The Southwestern Pacific Rim

In this region, the natural landscape is the most compelling source of color. South Seas images of swaying palm trees, curving beaches, and endless skies are nearly irresistible. Local flowers and birds may be the most colorful aspects of an island, and are as good a starting point for your palette as any. Forget big flowered prints. Hawaiian shirts are characteristic of Hawaii, not the entire South Pacific.

In the vast expanse of the Pacific between Hawaii and Australia lie thousands of inhabited islands. While the arts, crafts, and decorative traditions of these islands' peoples have common themes, color significance isn't one of them. Here, in the birthplace of the word taboo, there aren't any when it comes to color. Color is not symbolic or deeply meaningful in most traditional decorative crafts. There are, nonetheless, characteristic uses of color, some specific to certain islands or groups of islands. The South Pacific, also known as Oceana, is typically divided into two sectors, Polynesia and Melanesia.

Polynesia is the triangle between Hawaii, New Zealand, and Easter Island. The most prominent islands and groups of this region are Samoa, Tahiti, and Tonga. Most art involves the carving of totems symbolic of ancestors and animals, or the decoration of functional objects. Where color is used, it is for purely decorative purposes, limited only by the ingredients available.

There are two types of cloth produced in Polynesia that are useful reference points for the region's color use. Tahitian quilts, called tifaifai, are of contrasting colors, and usually decorated with a floral design or a repeating geometric pattern. The finished quilt is given and used for special occasions; it may be a bedspread for newlyweds, or a cover for a coffin. Tapa, made in Tonga, is a felt-like, multipurpose cloth dyed into mellow rust, red-orange, and yellow hues. Designs and patterns are purely decorative.

The lustrous black pearls cultivated in the region are a point of pride and an important element of the local economy. The pale, golden brown sand of picture postcards isn't found on Tahiti, where the volcanic sand is black or dark brown.

Melanesia is composed of the islands of the Western South Pacific that stretch from Fiji to New Guinea, and include New Caledonia and the Solomons. In contrast to Polynesia, Melanesia has a long tradition of decorating everyday objects in bright colors, which predates the arrival of European and American items (which are now commonplace).

Tongan Tapa cloth is always red and black, but each color might be in a wide variety of shades depending upon the whims and preferences of the maker. Unlike the Maori of New Zealand, the people of Fiji and Tonga have no folklore about the local reptiles. The indigenous banded iguanas are a sharp emerald green. The males also sport bluish-gray bands across their backs. These creatures change color, getting darker in direct sunlight in order to maintain their internal temperature.

Australia, New Zealand, and The Philippines

Australia
Australia's flag bears the British influence, with a small version of the Union Jack in the corner. The flag's seven stars are symbolic There's one for each of the six states and one for Australia's territories.

New Zealand
New Zealand's flag is much like that of Australia. The red in this flag (as in the stars) is particularly significant, since it is such an important color to the Maori who inhabit New Zealand.

The Philippines
A yellow starburst in a triangle of white sits at one end of the Philippine flag, and equal-sized bands of red and blue run horizontally across the rest of it. The flag is displayed often with both patriotic fervor and crass commercial intent; not quite as ubiquitous as the American Stars and Stripes, but close.

The Australian landscape and native culture greatly influences its aesthetic.

The color conventions of the British Isles came to Australia with the first European settlers. While British traditions, including those to do with color, still hold sway, the impact of the Australian landscape has been momentous, and the unique and exotic geography of the continent captures the imagination and defines the Australian aesthetic. The aboriginal palette of black, white, earthy reds, and ochre comes from native soil and minerals. This is tied to the sunlight-induced color changes of Ayers Rock that have helped make it a sacred spot to Australian Aborigines. It is composed of arkosic sandstone that takes on dramatically different shades of red-orange throughout the day, especially at sunrise and sunset; it can turn white, black, or purplish during and after a rainstorm. Ayers Rock, and the vast tracks of the Outback, trump anything manmade (with the possible exception of the Sydney Opera House) for top landmark status.

For the native Maori, the colors of New Zealand with the greatest resonance are red and green.

Like Australia, New Zealand's colonizers brought the customary color meanings of their primarily British homelands with them. The feathers of colorful birds—the brighter the better—were often used for personal adornment and to decorate everyday items. Multicolored cloaks made from parrot feathers were woven into elaborate rectilinear patterns and highly valued. A small bundle of feathers tied to a gourd labeled the contents according to some family specific color-coding of foodstuffs. The tail feathers—long black with a white tip at the end—of the rare huia bird were so valuable that they were kept in "feather boxes," specially made for these prized objects.

The Philippine aesthetic sensibility reflects a mix of outside influences.

More Latino than Asian, the Philippines seem almost out of place in Asia; it is the only Catholic country in the region, sharing more of a cultural heritage with their colonial cousins in Mexico than neighboring archipelagos in the South China Sea. The people of this country are said to have "Malaysian faces, Spanish names, and American vocabularies." The country's aesthetic sensibility—among other things—reflects this mixture.

Filipinos don't follow any particular system of color meaning or methodology, although the influences of several are clearly evident (see Catholic Colors, Spain, Mexico, and Central America). The islands' status as a regional backwater dulled the effects of contact with the rest of Asia. Colonized by Spain in the 16th century, the Philippines—on the opposite side of the globe from the Spanish Imperial throne—were administered via Mexico, making them virtually a colony of a colony. As a consequence, Mexico's attitudes, culture, style, and colors had more impact than Spain's. The look of various Filipino folk crafts' styles and patterns are sometimes indistinguishable from their counterparts in Central America. The bold green, red, and yellow stripes of the traditional Mexican serape would seem right at home amid any display of the colorful decorative arts of the Philippines.

The United States took possession of the Philippines at the beginning of the 20th century, granting them independence in 1946. A local saying has it that the Philippines spent "400 years in a convent, then fifty years in Hollywood." Successive waves of American military personnel stationed in the Philippines ensured a steady stream of up-to-the-minute American tastes, trends, and products.

Bamboo World is Australia's bamboo botanical garden, meant to promote non-invasive bamboo. This sub-tropical seventy-seven acre site has more than one thousand bamboo plants. Tan is also the color of wild camels, which can be found only in Australia. It helps to know that Australia is the driest inhabited continent in the world, which explains the preponderance of dusty browns and tans found here.

The Great Barrier Reef is the largest coral reef in the world. It is made up of two parts   multicolored coral, which consists of living polyps, and white coral, which is made up of the bodies of countless polyps that have died over hundreds of thousands of years.

Many different kinds of fish inhabit the Great Barrier Reef, including the orange-and-white-striped tomato clown fish.

Traditional Maori weaving used an ochre and straw-yellow color theme.

The color of Easter, with its strong associations of resurrection and rebirth, yellow became the color of the Philippines' People Power movement that overthrew Ferdinand Marcos in the 1980s.

THE JEEPNEY

The best, and best-known, example of the Filipino's exuberant decoration is the jeepney. Filipinos converted leftover US Army jeeps into hybrid taxi/bus vehicles that are the island's primary form of mass transit. Drivers wildly adorned their jeepneys in celebration of independence, and then never stopped. Jeepneys come in wild colors, and are covered in stripes, geometric designs, cartoon art, emblems, stickers, and slogans on the side, top, hood, and hanging from the windows. Attachments don't stop at the one-dimensional there may be lights of all kinds, tassles, a herd of hood ornaments, and a frieze of saints along the dashboard. An annual competition gives awards for the most original and elaborately decorated jeepney.

Uluru (Ayers Rock) is a huge rock in the Outback that is six miles around (nine kilometers) and 100 feet high (348 meters). It changes color from mauve to blue to pink to brown to fiery red as the sunlight moves across it. The Devil's Marbles, massive boulders found along the Outback's Stuart Highway, also take on a red glow at sunset.

Among New Zealand's indigenous Maori people, bright and vivid reds were sacred and reserved for gods and chiefs. In traditional Maori houses, exposed beams were painted with spiral geometric patters in white on an earthy red background. The soil of much of New Zealand is ruddy and reddish dust eventually tints almost everything.

It's impossible not to think of blue when thinking of Australia, as the island is famous for its beaches and water sports. Blue is the dominant color of the flags of the South Pacif

Talismans and symbols of protection were worn as pendants carved of greenstone, the local variety of jade. Green was not always positive, however. Lizards were considered emissaries of lesser evil spirits. Their presence could mean that a demon was trying to kill you. At the same time, lizards were guardians of the dead, a threat to anyone who would defile a grave; carved images of lizards mark sacred places.

Due to Mexico's influence when the Philippines were colonized, green is a common color in handmade crafts.

The Chocolate Hills are the most famous attraction in Bohol in the Philippines. They are so named because the green grass that covers them turns brown in the summer.

In the Philippines' Black Nazarene procession, the largest procession in the country, a life-size blackwood statue of Jesus is carried through the streets of Quiapo.

■ ■ ■ Despite Australia's varied geography and lengths of coastline, it is the mythic and forbidding terrain of the Outback that has become the country's iconic landscape. For a brochure introducing a promotional trip to Australia, American designer John Sayles started with the Outback's khaki and green color scheme, added imagery inspired by aboriginal art, and printed the job on brown chipboard to reinforce the rough and tumble wilderness adventure aspect of the destination.

PROJECT   AUSTRALIAN TRIP PROMOTIONAL BROCHURE
DESIGN FIRM   SAYLES GRAPHIC DESIGN
ART DIRECTOR   JOHN SAYLES

The brown and blue of the identity system for Globe
Studio reflects the brown of the earth and the blue of
the sky in the expansive territory of Australia.

PROJECT	GLOBE STUDIO IDENTITY
DESIGN FIRM	MOTHER GRAPHIC DESIGN
ART DIRECTOR/	
DESIGNER	KRISTIN THIEME
CLIENT	GLOBE STUDIO

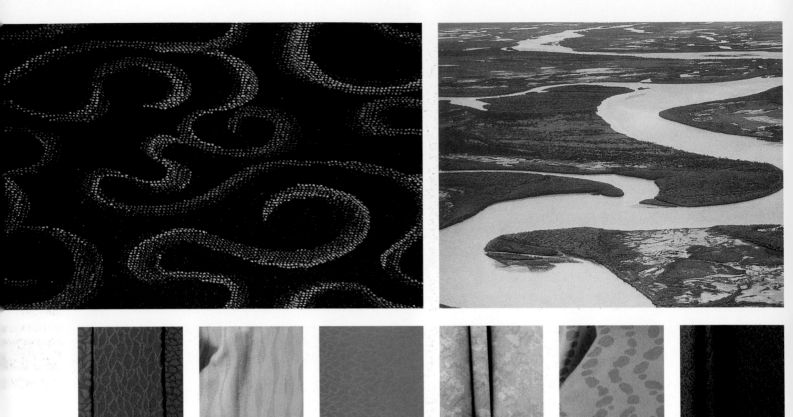

■ ■ ■ ■ ■ Quantas Airways retained Cato Partners to develop the graphics for the airline's cabin interior fabrics, bulkhead wallpaper, and print collateral. Designers found their inspiration for the project in the Australian landscape, interestingly as seen from the perspective of a Quantas customer in flight. Aerial photographs of the terrain showed Australia's unique color and texture, which designers adapted as the dominant graphics in the cabin upholstery, wallpaper, blankets, and lounge interiors featuring rich shades of blues and blue-green along with a palette of tan, gold, and brown.

PROJECT   QUANTAS AIRWAYS' GRAPHICS
DESIGN FIRM CATO PARTNERS
DESIGNER   CATO PARTNERS
CLIENT   QUANTAS AIRWAYS

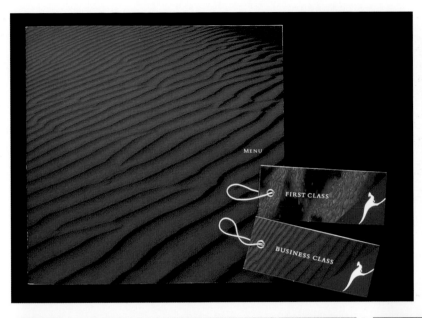

Resources

United Nations

The United Nations Educational, Scientific, and Cultural Organization (UNESCO) maintains a lending library of about 150,000 volumes of publications printed by UNESCO and other international organizations concerned with education, science, culture, communication, social sciences, and human sciences.

UNESCO Library
7 Place de Fontenoy
75352 Paris 07 SP FRANCE
Phone   (33) 1 45 68 19 57
Fax   (33) 1 45 68 56 17

Consulate Offices

To obtain up-to-date information about the culture, customs, tourism, and protocol for a particular nation, contact that country's local embassy. Consulate offices are located in major cities around the world where diplomatic relations have been established such as New York, Chicago, San Francisco, Toronto, Vancouver, London, Paris, Hong Kong, and Tokyo. The following is a list of missions established in New York.

Consulate General of Argentina
12 W. 56th St.
New York, NY 10019
212/603-0400

Australian Consulate General
150 East 42nd St.
33rd Fl.
New York, NY 10017
212/408-8400

Austrian Consulate General
31 E. 69th St.
New York, NY 10021
212/737-6400

Consulate of The Bahamas
231 E. 46nd St.
New York, NY 10017
212/421-6420

Consulate General of Belgium
50 Rockefeller Plaza
New York, NY 10020
212/586-5110

Consulate General of Brazil
551 5th Ave.
New York, NY 10176
212/916-3200

British Consulate General
845 3rd Ave., 10th Fl.
New York, NY 10022
212/745-0202

Consulate General Du Canada
1251 Avenue of the Americas
New York, NY 10020
212/596-1783

Consulate General of Chili
866 UN Plaza, #302
New York, NY 10017
212/980-3366

Consulate General of Colombia
10 E. 46th St.
New York, NY 10017
212/949-9898

Consulate General of Costa Rica
80 Wall St.
New York, NY 10005
212/425-2620

Cyprus Consulate General of the Republic
13 E. 40th St.
New York, NY 10016
212/686-6016

Consulate General of Denmark
Dag Hammarskjold Plaza
New York, NY 10017
212/223-4545

Consulate General of France
934 5th Ave.
New York, NY 10021
212/606-3600

Consulate General of Germany
871 United Nations Plaza
New York, NY 10017
212/610-9700

Greek Consulate General
69 E. 79th St.
New York, NY 10021
212/988-5500

Consulate General of India
3 E. 64th St.
New York, NY 10021
212/774-0600

Consulate General of Indonesia
5 E. 68th St.
New York, NY 10021
212/879-0600

Consulate General of Ireland
345 Park Ave., 17th Fl.
New York, NY 10154
212/319-2555

Consulate General of Israel
800 Second Ave.
New York, NY 10017
212/499-5000

Consulate of Italy
690 Park Ave.
New York, NY 10021
212/737-9100

Jamaica Consulate General
767 Third Ave.
New York, NY 10017
212/935-9000

Consulate General of Japan
299 Park Ave, 19th Fl.
New York, NY 10171
212/371-8222

Kenya Consulate
424 Madison Ave.
New York, NY 10017
212/486-1300

Consulate General of South Korea
460 Park Ave. South.
New York, NY 10016
212/752-1700

Consulate General of Malaysia
313 E. 43rd St.
New York, NY 10017
212/490-2722

Consulate General of Mexico
8 E. 41st St.
New York, NY 10017
212/689-0456

Consulate General of Monaco
565 5th Ave.
New York, NY 10017
212/286-0500

Consulate General of Morocco
10 E. 40th St.
New York, NY 10016
212/758-2625

Consulate General of Nepal
820 2nd Ave.
New York, NY 10017
212/370-4188

Consulate General of The Netherlands
1 Rockefeller Plaza, 11th Fl.
New York, NY 10020
212/246-1429

Consulate General of Norway
825 3d Ave.
New York, NY 10022
212/421-7333

Consulate General of Pakistan
12 E. 65th St.
New York, NY 10021
212/879-5800

Consulate General of The People's
Republic of China
520 12th Ave.
New York, NY 10036
212/330-7400

Consulate General of Poland
233 Madison Ave.
New York, NY 10016
212/889-8360

Consulate General of Portugal
630 Fifth Ave.
New York, NY 10111
212/765-2980

Russian Consulate General
9 E. 91st St.
New York, NY 10128
212/348-0926

Singapore Mission to the UN
231 E. 51st St.
New York, NY 10022
212/223-3331

Consulate General of Spain
150 E. 58th St.
New York, NY 10155
212/355-4080

Consulate General of Sweden
885 Second Ave, 45th Fl.
New York, NY 10017
212/583-2550

Consulate General of Switzerland
663 3rd Ave.
New York, NY 10017
212/599-5700

Thai Consulate General
351 E. 52nd St.
New York, NY 10022
212/754-1770

Consulate General of Turkey
821 UN Plaza, 5th Fl.
New York, NY 10017
212/949-0160

Directory of Contributors

Ana Couto Design
Rua Joana Angélica 173
3° andar
Ipanema 22420-030
Rio de Janeiro
Brazil
acgd@anacouto-design.com.br

Beylea
1809 7th Avenue, Suite 1250
Seattle, WA 98101
www.belyea.com

Boelts Bros. Associates
345 East University Boulevard
Tucson, AZ 85705
bba@boelts-bros.com

Bonsey Design Partnership
179 River Valley Road
Level 5, Unit 1 R.V. Building
Singapore 179033
jonathan@bonsey.com

Bruno/Garrie Faget
Avenida Las Heras 2352 3rd 20
Buenos Aires 1425
Argentina
bruno&garrie@interar.com.ar

Braue Design
Eiswerkestrasse 8
27572 Bremerhaven
Germany
info@brauedesign.de

Cato Partners
254 Swan Street
Richmond 3121
Victoria, Australia
chairman@cato.com.au

Carré Noir
Rue des Mimosasstraat, 44
B-1030 Brussels
Belgium

Carter Wong and Partners
29 Brook Mews North
London W2 3BW
United Kingdom

Cartlidge Levine
238 St. John Street
London EC1V 4PH
United Kingdom
Telephone (+44) 171-252-6608

Clic Limited
Kornhill Metro Tower
1 Kornhill Road, Suite 801
Quarry Bay
Hong Kong
Clic@clic.com.hk

Designation Inc.
53 Spring Street
New York, NY 10012
mikequon@aol.com

Desgrippes Gobé & Associates
411 Lafayette Street, 2nd Floor
New York, NY 10003
www.dga.com

Erwin Zinger Graphic Design
Bunnemaheerd 68
9737 RE Groningen
The Netherlands
Erwin_zinger@hotmail.com

Fabrice Praeger
54 Bis Rue de L'Ermitage
7520 Paris
France

5D Studio
20651 Seaboard Road
Malibu, CA 90215
Jane5D@aol.com

Frame Graphics Co., Ltd.
1-13-15 #4F Jinnan
Shibuyaku, Tokyo
Japan
tanaka@framegraphics.co.jp

Gottschalk + Ash International
Böcklinstrasse 26
8032 Zurich
Switzerland
gottashintl@access.ch

Greteman Group
1425 East Douglas Avenue
Wichita, KS 67211
Sgreteman@gretemangroup.com

Henry Wolf Productions
167 East 73rd Street
New York, NY 10021

HGV Design Consultants
46A Roseberry Avenue
London EC7R 4RP
United Kingdom
Design@hgv.co.uk

Ian Logan Design Company
42 Charterhouse Square
London EC1 M6EU
England
ildc@ildc.demon.co.uk

Incognito Design Oy
Töölönkatu 11
FIN-00100, Helsinki
Finland
info@incognito.fi

Interbrand Avalos & Bourse
La Pampa 1351 Capital Federal
Argentina
Cavalos@avalosbourse.com.ar

Javier Romero Design Group
24 East 23rd Street, Third Floor
New York, NY 10010
javierr@jrdg.com

João Machado Design, Lda.
Rua Padre Xavier Coutinho, n° 125-4150-751
Porto
Portugal
www.joaomachado.com

Kan & Lau Design Consultants
28/F Great Smart Tower
230 Wanchai Road
Hong Kong
China
Kan@kanandlau.com

Lewis Moberly
33 Gresse Street
London W1P 2LP
United Kingdom
lewismoberly@enterprise.net

Lieber Brewster Design, Inc.
19 W. 34th Street, #618
New York, NY 10001
lieber@interport.net

Mike Salisbury Communications Inc.
4223 Glencoe Avenue
Marina Del Rey, CA 90292
mikesalcom@aol.com

Mires Design, Inc.
2345 Kettner Boulevard
San Diego, CA 92101
www.miresdesign.com

Miriello Grafico, Inc.
419 West G Street
San Diego, CA 92101
chris@miriellografico.com

Mires Design, Inc.
2345 Kettner Boulevard
San Diego, CA 92101
www.miresdesign.com

Miriello Grafico, Inc.
419 West G Street
San Diego, CA 92101
chris@miriellografico.com

Muriel Paris et Alex Singer
20 rue Dautancourt
75017 Paris
France
Parism@worldnet.fr

Nakajima Design Co., Ltd.
Kaiho Building, 4F
4-11, Uguisudani-cho
Sibuya-ku, Tokyo 150-0032
Japan
Nkjm-d@kd5.so-net.ne.jp

Orange
402-1008 Homer Street
Vancouver, British Columbia V6B 2X1
Canada
Pulp@istar.ca

Plazm Media
P.O. Box 2863
Portland, OR 97208-2863
Josh@plazm.com

R2 Design
Praceta D. Nuno Álvares Pereira
20-5° FQ
4450-218 Matosinhos
Portugal
R2design@mail.telepac.pt

RTKL Associates Inc.
One South Street
Baltimore, MD 21206

Rigsby Design
2309 University Boulevard
Houston, TX 77005
Lrigsby@rigsby.com

Rullkötter AGD
Kleines Heenfeld 19
D-32278 Kirchlengern
Germany
Info@rullkoetter.de

Sagmeister Inc.
222 West 14 Street, #15A
New York, NY 10011
Ssagmeister@aol.com

Sayles Graphic Design
3701 Beaver Avenue
Des Moines, IA 50310
Sayles@saylesdesign.com

Source/Inc.
116 South Michigan Avenue
Chicago, IL 60603
wjoconnor@sourcedesign.com

Starbucks Coffee Company
Starbucks Design Group
2401 Utah Avenue S.
Seattle, WA 98134

Selbert Perkins Design
2067 Massachusetts Avenue
Cambridge, MA 02140

Studio GT & P
Via Ariosto,
5-06034 Foligno (PG)
Italy
Gt&p@cline.it

Studio Karavil
Corso di P.Ticinese 50
20123 Milano
Italy
Bessikaravil@tin.it

Supon Design Group
1700 K Street NW, #400
Washington, DC 20006
suponp@supon.com

Swieter Design US
3227 McKinney Avenue, #201
Dallas, TX 75204
graphics@swieter.com

Terrapin Graphics
991 Avenue Road
Toronto, Ontario M5P 2K9
Canada
James@terrapin-graphics.com

The Observer Magazine
119 Farringdon Road
London EC1R 3ER
United Kingdom
Wayne.ford@observer.co.uk

30sixty design, inc.
2801 Cahuenga Boulevard West
Los Angeles, CA 90068

3 Ring Circus
1857 Taft Avenue
Los Angeles, CA 90028

Vrontikis Design Office
2021 Pontius Avenue
Los Angeles, CA 90025-5613
pv@35k.com

WPA Pinfold
Ex Libris, Nineveh Road, Holbeck
Leeds LS11 9Q9
United Kingdom
design@wpa-pinfold.co.uk

Yfactor, Inc.
2020 Clark Boulevard, Suite 1B
Brampton, Ontario L6T 5R4
Canada
Info@yfactor.com

The Authors

L. K. Peterson is a writer and design journalist. A former graphic designer and illustrator, he has been an editor at *Metropolitan Home* and CitySports magazines and *Fodor's* travel guides. His recent books include *Passport USA, A Guide to American Customs and Etiquette, The Trucker's Road Atlas,* and *the USA Today Four Sports Stadium Guide.*

Cheryl Dangel Cullen is a writer and public relations consultant specializing in the graphic arts industry. She is the author of *Graphic Design Resource Photography, The Best of Annual Report Design,* and *The Best of Direct Response Graphics.* Cullen writes from her home near Ann Arbor, Michigan, where she plans and implements public relations programs for clients in the graphic arts, paper, and printing industries. She frequently gives presentations and seminars on innovative ways to push the creative edge in design using a variety of substrates.